D1612943

Chance and Intent

This compact and readable book will help executives, entrepreneurs, and venture investors learn to search out and plan for those enterprise hazards that reside outside the bell curve, the conventional domain of risk, including:

- Uncertainty, where outcomes can be characterized in advance but reliable estimates cannot be made for the likelihood that they will occur;
- Ambiguity, where the events and outcomes cannot be well characterized, in some cases because we cannot imagine them and in others because characterization depends upon the institutional interests or cultural values of the observer; and
- Ignorance, where neither likelihood estimates nor well-characterized events enjoy much credibility.

This brief volume emphasizes practical strategies for understanding and managing the hazards of the new venture in light of recent research. It will help corporate innovators, entrepreneurs, and investors employ a wider spectrum of risk management strategies than is now possible.

David L. Bodde serves as Professor of Engineering at the International Center for Automotive Research, Clemson University. His current research and teaching address open-architecture innovation processes and their implications for risk management. He serves on the boards of private equity and publicly traded companies.

Caron H. St. John is Dean of the College of Business Administration at the University of Alabama in Huntsville. She has published in leading scholarly journals including *Academy of Management Review, Strategic Management Journal, Journal of Operations Management, Production and Operations Management,* and *Organizational Research Methods,* as well as two textbooks on strategic management. She teaches undergraduate and graduate courses that address the business, operations, and technology strategies of firms.

Chance and Intent

Managing the Risks of Innovation
and Entrepreneurship

Edited by

David L. Bodde
and Caron H. St. John

Routledge
Taylor & Francis Group

NEW YORK AND LONDON

First published 2012
by Routledge
711 Third Avenue, New York, NY 10017

Simultaneously published in the UK
by Routledge
2 Park Square, Milton Park, Abingdon, Oxon OX14 4RN

Routledge is an imprint of the Taylor & Francis Group, an informa business

Library of Congress Cataloging-in-Publication Data
Chance and intent: managing the risks of innovation and entrepreneurship/
  [edited by] David L. Bodde and Caron H. St. John.
    p. cm.
    Includes index.
    I1. Entrepreneurship. 2. Venture capital. 3. Technological innovations
    —Economic aspects. 4. New products. 5. Risk management. I. Bodde,
    David L. II. St. John, Caron H.
    HB615.C527 2011
    658.4—dc23
    2011036246

ISBN: 978-0-415-87760-2 (hbk)
ISBN: 978-0-415-87761-9 (pbk)
ISBN: 978-0-203-12667-7 (ebk)

Typeset in Bell Gothic
by Florence Production Ltd, Stoodleigh, Devon

Printed and bound in Great Britain by
CPI Antony Rowe, Chippenham, Wiltshire

Contents

Acknowledgments

No book project is accomplished by authors and editors alone, but *Chance and Intent* benefitted especially from the generosity of others. Most fundamentally, the project was enabled by a generous grant from the Ewing Marion Kauffman Foundation. In particular, we appreciate Dr. Robert J. Strom of the Kauffman Foundation for his wise counsel and patience during this lengthy process. Without both, this project would not exist.

Those colleagues who contributed chapters to *Chance and Intent* deserve special recognition. Setting aside time to thoughtfully address the intersection of fortune and design surely required some sacrifice of personal time for which we are grateful. In order of appearance, the chapter authors include: Philip Bromiley, Devaki Rau, William B. Gartner, Jianwen Liao, Rita Gunther McGrath, Jeffrey Pfeffer, John T. Wilbanks, James A. Euchner, and Robert Laubacher.

The early work benefitted from the support and encouragement of the Arthur M. Spiro Institute for Entrepreneurial Leadership at Clemson University. The Institute was established with a generous gift from textile industry leader and entrepreneur Arthur M. Spiro and his wife, Joan. In addition, Dr. Bruce Yandle, then Dean of the College of Business and Behavioral Sciences at Clemson, provided support and wise leadership.

To the extent that this volume offers clear and graceful expression, we must thank Dr. Elizabeth Clay, whose withering disdain for passive voice and "to be" verbs informed the writing and editing. To the extent that it does not, we have only ourselves to blame. In addition, we appreciate Arch Coal, Inc. for contributing to the scenario analysis case presented in Chapter 5. In particular, Chairman and CEO Steven F. Leer and Vice President, Human Resources, Sheila Feldman gave generously of their time and advice. Any errors remain ours.

We owe special appreciation to Aindreela Dutt Bodde, whose thoughtful and creative design graces the book's cover. And finally we must thank our families for whom the chores of organizing, editing, and writing took the place of movies, ball games, model airplane building, or just hanging out. We were not the only ones to bear the price of authorship.

DAVID L. BODDE
Clemson, South Carolina
CARON H. ST. JOHN
Huntsville, Alabama

Introduction: Some Thoughts at the Beginning Concerning Risk and its Management

There is nothing more difficult to take in hand, more perilous to conduct or more uncertain in its success than to take the lead in the introduction of a new order of things.

Niccolo Machiavelli 1515

IT DOES SEEM UNFAIR that innovation and entrepreneurship, those great engines of human progress, should be among the riskiest of human endeavors. But if life were better arranged, there would be no need for this book. *Chance and Intent* invites independent entrepreneurs, corporate innovators, and venture investors to consider new ways to manage the risks that necessarily accompany the new enterprise—not as an afterthought, nor as filler for the obligatory sections of their business plan software, but as a fully integrated part of the business design.

By "entrepreneurs and innovators" we mean those seeking to introduce a new order of things through high-potential, technology-based ventures, either operating independently or from the platform of an established company (or not-for-profit). We view successful entrepreneurship as a behavioral trait, and those behaviors can be practiced in a variety of organizational settings including that of the investor. We find the term "risk" used in multiple ways by multiple analysts and practitioners— and sometimes by the same analyst/practitioner. For our purposes, we will just speak of risk conversationally—a general descriptor for the chance that misfortune or mistake will overtake the new venture.

CHESTERTON'S DILEMMA: HOW MUCH RISK CAN REALLY BE MANAGED?

The English writer and philosopher G. K. Chesterton once observed the essential dilemma of risk: that life is not illogical, yet it sets a trap for those relying purely on logic; that the world looks just a bit more mathematical and regular than it really is; and that life's exactitude is obvious, but its inexactitude hides in wait of the unwary. This sets before us a dilemma: can risk really be managed? Or are we simply comforting ourselves with analytical rituals of no greater significance than reading chicken entrails?

Pre-industrial civilizations might well have taken the latter view, had it occurred to them to ask the question at all. Not that risk was unknown to the ancients, but rather that to them it generally meant ill fortune originating in acts of nature or the caprice of minor deities. Games of chance, apparently popular from the dawn of civilization, provided the chief venue and the motivation for any analysis.

But the emergence of industrial society and the more complex and interactive organizations that attended it gave rise to the notion that risk could be managed in some manner that improves the likelihood that the new venture will succeed. Consider, for example, the rise of that decisive legal innovation, the corporation, in the eighteenth and nineteenth centuries. Two features of the corporate form of organization sharpened and focused the search for better ways to understand and manage risk. The first is the separation of ownership and management with outside investors financing the investments of the firm. How can owners have confidence in the risks being undertaken on their behalf—a question as compelling in the world of private finance and venture capital as in public companies? The second is the invention of limited liability in which the corporation assumes responsibility for its own actions, thus limiting the loss for investors and managers. Shielded from personal responsibility (apart from breaking the law), will companies operate in ways that pass on risk to the general public—as in "too big to fail" or as in environmental pollution?

Thus, the rise of risk management sprang in part from necessity. Indeed, the transition toward a closely coupled, international society built on technological change and capital investment could not have gone far without it. Equally important, the art of risk management arose from the opportunity for choice. Human organizations enjoy the privilege of intentional choice: decisions about goals, incentives, structure, and strategy, all of which are the stuff of management. These decisions can mitigate or amplify the risks of entrepreneurial ventures. Yet the larger world offering risks outside management's control remains unknowable and unmanageable. Monetary inflation, war, natural disaster, technology breakthroughs, and the like can strongly influence the risk of any new venture. The best plans of mice and men are really about equal.

PRACTICAL WISDOM FOR THE CAT'S DILEMMA

American humorist Mark Twain once observed that a cat that once sits on a hot stove lid will never sit on a hot stove lid again—but neither will it sit on a cold stove lid. Similarly, the only way to eliminate the risks of a new venture is to not attempt it at all. But abstinence applied to innovation and entrepreneurship is like abstinence applied to procreation—things eventually grind to a halt without it. Witness the fate of the old Soviet Union, which suffered greatly from the conceit that risk could be removed entirely from society by proper planning and central direction. And so if our post-industrial society can't afford to quit, then it had better learn to win. The central issue is how to do that.

Chance and Intent is written for practitioners, those who choose to take the lead in creating a new order of things. It seeks to make available fresh research and thinking about risk, and especially how it can be managed in a way that helps control the hazards of the new venture. We organize this around three chief sources of risk: (a) risks arising from the human propensities of entrepreneurial decision-making; (b) risks arising from an unruly, external business environment; and, (c) risks of new forms of innovation—networks, open innovation models, crowdsourcing, and the like.

Part I, "Decision-Making Under Stress and Uncertainty" addresses the decision-making propensities of the team launching the new ventures. However skilled, however experienced, however wise the team might be, as individuals and collectively, they remain heir to all the follies of humankind. Part I speaks to these decision-making foibles, the role they play in risk, and what innovators, entrepreneurs, and their investors can do to manage them.

But neither the management team nor its investors are completely in charge. And so, we must deal with the second source of difficulty, hazards that arise from the business environment—the set of forces beyond the direct reach of a new venture and its employees, but strongly affecting the business. Think, for example, of the world price of oil, whose volatility provides a strong tail wind, a strong head wind, and sometimes both in turn for a host of opportunities. These are the "Unruly Realities" of Part II. And third, we must consider risks arising from new modes of innovation, especially open-source and network innovation, which offer unfamiliar opportunities and threats to the new venture. These emerging risks are the "New Horizons" of Part III.

But genius stumbles, luck runs out, and our best management cannot prevent some failures. The received wisdom of research and development managers holds that of every 10 serious research ideas, on average only one actually achieves commercial introduction. The batting average of professional venture capital is not much better. And so our brief tour of risk would be incomplete without consideration of failure, which like risk is a thing to be managed.

WHEN TO HOLD AND WHEN TO FOLD: FAILURE AS AN OPTION

A popular T-shirt slogan holds that "Failure is not an option," and there are actually places where this is true—if at first you don't succeed, you might reconsider taking up skydiving. Similarly, no air traveler wants to fly with an air traffic control system that learns by trial and error. But operating the air traffic control system is not about creating a new order of things. Rather it enables others to achieve that by ensuring safe stewardship of the existing order. For those who invent the future, innovators and entrepreneurs, failure is not merely an option but a necessity. This is true for several reasons.

First, the term "failure" itself implies that a correct solution exists, but that you failed to find it. In air traffic control, this is exactly the case. But in creating new ventures, many solutions can be discerned at the beginning—all of apparently equal promise, each with a plausible story. Reasoning from first principles helps, but the analysis soon reaches its limits. To proceed farther without new information builds the entire enterprise upon a foundation of supposition, logically correct but factually wrong. And so the only way to elicit new information is to try something, to master the art of the cheap experiment. Wise, low-cost experiments can fail to deliver the anticipated results, but they will never fail to deliver the information needed to move forward with the venture. The core idea is to "fail fast, fail cheap, fail forward."

None of this argues for a vulgar empiricism. Rather, it argues that an unknowable future holds surprises for the most discerning analysts. Thus the future does not belong to those who know the most about the present, but rather to those who can gain the most accurate perspective on the future—those with the keenest learning skills. The fundamental purpose of this book is to help corporate innovators and entrepreneurs master those learning skills.

WHAT'S IN A NAME?

A book's title should be more than a mere label, but rather should capture the central theme of the work. We have attempted to accomplish that in *Chance and Intent* by striking an holistic balance between managing risk and managing all the other components of innovation and entrepreneurship. Consider two vignettes.

> Some years ago, a prominent clearinghouse for magazine subscriptions sought to increase sales by promoting a million-dollar prize sweepstakes. About every six months, an oversized envelope would show up in the mailbox with photos of prize winners squealing with delight at the announcement. Presumably, recipients of these blandishments would be more inclined to part with a few bucks for a magazine, secure in the hope that they would be the next winner. One of your editors, bemused by the prize—and we refuse to say whom—would regularly send in a sweepstakes entry without much consideration of the likelihood of winning. This practice persisted despite the realization that the expected value of the prize was not worth the postage required to send it, let alone the time required to complete the forms without inadvertently purchasing a magazine. And so a focus on *Intent* without due consideration of the prospects for achieving it wastes time and resources.
>
> But similarly, excessive attention to risk, the *Chance* that the venture will go wrong, can become a recipe for inaction—the "paralysis by analysis" legendary among defense analysts. Consider, for example, General George B. McClellan, by any measure a brilliant Civil War strategist and organizer, but hesitant and indecisive on the battlefield. During the Peninsula Campaign of 1862, a story is told of a reconnaissance in which McClellan and his senior staff were paused beside a creek bank. The debate was the depth of the water,

and hence whether to risk fording by foot soldiers. Exasperated by the fruitless speculation, a young cavalry Captain rode his horse into the creek until the water reached his stirrups. Turning in the saddle to McClellan, the Captain said, "Sir, it is *this* deep." The Captain was George Armstrong Custer, often accused of many things, but never of paying excessive attention to risk.

PART I

Decision-Making Under Stress and Uncertainty

. . . don't let the sound of your own wheels make you crazy.

Jackson Brown

POOR DECISIONS BY SMART, capable people mark the history of all human endeavor, and this is no less true for entrepreneurs and innovators. This opening section of *Chance and Intent* seeks ways to understand and to manage the idiosyncrasies of that most difficult of human activities, wise decision-making.

Two kinds of pressures strongly influence human judgment, and we must understand both if we are to attempt to manage them. The first arises from the idiosyncrasies of individual behavior: our decisions are biased by the many small irrationalities that separate human judgments from those that would be made by a rational actor . . . or a robot. The story of the doomed polar expedition of the British explorer Sir Ernest Shackleton, which follows, illustrates the foibles of individual decision-making for good and for ill.

The second pressure is organizational. Decisions are rarely made outside the context of some institution, whether it be a small startup, major corporation, or government agency. The culture of the organization within which decisions must be made strongly influences the choices of the decision-makers. The fatal decision to launch the space shuttle *Challenger*, also following, illustrates the influence of organizational context.

ERROR AND RESILIENCE: SHACKLETON'S LAST POLAR EXPEDITION

Judgments of risk and return must eventually be made by individuals, and so their decision-making propensities bear examination. Consider the case of Sir Ernest Shackleton, an Antarctic explorer who never fully achieved the promises made to investors in any of his explorations. His final expedition, which set out in 1914 to trek from one side of Antarctica to the other via the South Pole, never set foot on the continent. Instead, an error in judgment left his ship, *Endurance*, trapped offshore in the ice floe and eventually crushed by it. Yet the story of how Shackleton led his entire team to safety remains today an exemplar of resilient decision-making and leadership.

The exploration industry was a thriving, keenly competitive enterprise as the nineteenth century rolled into the twentieth. Entrepreneurial explorers raised funds from wealthy individuals (who got their names on mountains, promontories, and other recognizable topography), scientific societies (rewarded through their association with important discoveries), and governments (who got to plant the flag). Among the best of these was Sir Ernest Shackleton, and his chosen territory, the Antarctic, had become the focus of an international race to reach the South Pole. In 1895, the Sixth International Geographical Congress had convened in London to declare the Antarctic the most urgent scientific quest of the era.

Shackleton could offer impressive credentials to prospective financial supporters. He had gained experience as a member of Scott's 1901–2 expedition, which succeeded in getting closer to the Pole than any previous explorers. Around 1905, Shackleton began fund raising for another expedition, seeking a sum that would translate into the $3–5 million range in today's dollars. In good entrepreneurial fashion, he contacted a list of about 70 prominent London business persons, gained scientific credibility through the Royal Geographic Society, and used family connections to reach persons of influence and wealth. Seeking market space in the progressive Victorian mind, he even promised to use an automobile and motorized sledge on the ice—though common sense prevailed and these were later dropped.

The resulting 1907–8 expedition came within 100 miles of the South Pole, but turned back debilitated by hunger and frostbite. No doubt this disappointed Shackleton keenly. But this man of courage and intense competitive drive also possessed the good judgment to recognize an unacceptable risk—that continuing toward the Pole would cost the expedition their lives—and the humility to act responsibly on that knowledge. Though falling short of its goal, the Shackleton expedition did set a world record, which gained him a knighthood in 1909.

The race to the South Pole was won in 1911 by Norwegian explorer Roald Amundsen. This left Shackleton, who had been raising funds for another expedition, bereft of a compelling goal. Ever the entrepreneur, he soon conceived the next big thing—a transcontinental journey from sea to sea while crossing the Pole. Fund raising, however, proved difficult because both the Amundsen victory and the increasing prospect of war in Europe eclipsed Antarctic exploration in the public mind.

Nevertheless, Shackleton's persistence paid off. By the end of 1913, enough had been raised to procure supplies and a ship, named *Endurance* after the Shackleton family motto. *Endurance* departed a London dock just as England declared war on Germany in August of 1914.

The expedition arrived at South Georgia Island, the southernmost of Britain's whaling stations where Shackleton was advised by local captains that the ice floes that year had reached the most northerly point in memory. They strongly advised him that to sail risked becoming trapped in the ice. Shackleton waited a month on South Georgia. But when conditions failed to improve, the expedition departed for Antarctica in December of 1914 (midsummer in the Southern Hemisphere) betting on the triumph of audacity and good fortune over ill circumstance.

Making its way slowly through the thickening ice, *Endurance* had drawn within sight of the Antarctic shore when the floes closed all possibility of passage. Hopelessly trapped in the ice, the expedition would have to drift with the ice pack until it crushed the ship. And drift they did, generally northwest from January of 1915 when *Endurance* became trapped, until April of 1916 when they left the floe in lifeboats for Elephant Island, a barren, windswept rockpile just off the Antarctic continent. From there, Shackleton and a carefully selected crew sailed one of the boats 800 miles northeast to the whaling station at South Georgia, arriving there in May of 1916— one of the most remarkable feats of navigation and seamanship of all time. A rescue ship later recovered the remainder of the expedition from Elephant Island. All members of the expedition survived.

This meager telling does little justice to the saga, and far richer accounts are available (Lansing 1999). Instead, our purpose is to illustrate issues of individual decision-making in the face of high risk. These issues are the subject of Chapter 1 of Part I, "Managing an Entrepreneur's Risk-Taking Propensity." Drs. Philip Bromiley, Devaki Rau, and Caron H. St. John draw upon the work of psychologists and experimental economists to understand the idiosyncrasies of human behavior toward risk. Their synthesis sheds additional light on the Shackleton story.

For example, why would the normally prudent Shackleton make the enormous mistake of setting out from South Georgia despite the advice of experienced sailors familiar with the region? Though we cannot know his mind, the answer might be financial. Shackleton's personal credit was effectively ruined by over-extended loans he had taken out to finance the expedition. He must have known that any extended delay would require additional supplies, and he had every reason to believe that the financing to procure them would not be available. So rather than suffer the sure loss of the polar expedition, he took a gamble on the possibility of an even greater loss involving human suffering and possible death—a behavior entirely consistent with the observations of Bromiley, Rau, and St. John.

But why then did Shackleton's judgments become flawless once *Endurance* had been trapped by the closing ice? Each of his subsequent decisions—from abandoning the doomed *Endurance*, to the trek across the ice floes in search of open water, to the sail to Elephant Island, to the final sea crossing to South Georgia—proved to be well-conceived responses to desperate circumstances. Again, we must speculate.

But once all hope of the promised trans-polar trek had been lost, it appears that Shackleton's reference point had become survival and not mission accomplishment. And so from that point forward, every choice made was the least risky of a set of high-risk options, a conclusion entirely consistent with the behaviors set out by Bromiley, Rau, and St. John.

THE *CHALLENGER* LAUNCH DECISION: CULTURE AND THE NORMALIZATION OF DEVIANCE

We all know (or think we know) the public story—how mid-level managers at NASA and its contractor Thiokol over-rode the objections of knowledgeable engineers and decided to launch STS 51L that cold January morning in 1986. Lift-off occurred at 11:38 a.m. at a launch pad temperature of 36 degrees. Seventy-three seconds later the *Challenger* disappeared in a catastrophic explosion, and all seven of the crew perished.

The proximate cause was plain. The field joint that linked sections of the right solid rocket booster (SRB) had failed to contain the high pressure combustion gas. The zinc-chromate putty designed to seal the O-rings from the combustion gas failed to do so, and the resiliency of the O-rings themselves was impaired by the ambient cold. About 59 seconds after launch, a small flame became visible from the side of the SRB, and this impinged on the external tank containing the liquid hydrogen and oxygen fuels. At 73 seconds, the catastrophic explosion occurred.

Three major investigations followed quickly: one by a Presidential Commission led by former Attorney General William Rogers, one by the House Committee on Science and Technology, and one by NASA itself. From these investigations emerged the commonly understood narrative of the tragedy: that wrongdoing by mid-level managers seeking to maintain the launch schedule and hence the "productivity" of the shuttle system led to an otherwise preventable tragedy. Yet like so many historically accepted accounts, this narrative is incomplete and hence misleading. We must take time to understand the real lessons of the *Challenger* if we are to apply them to the risk of launching new ventures.

Such an understanding appears in a remarkable book, *The Challenger Launch Decision*, by Dr. Diane Vaughan (Vaughan 1996), and we will apply her conclusions about the NASA decision process to the risks of decision-making by new venture management teams. Vaughan's central point concerns the "normalization of deviance," by which she means the tendency of a culture—in this case that of NASA space flight operations—to ignore evidence that disconfirms the central theses of that culture. In the NASA of the 1980s, the central organizational thesis was that shuttle operations had become routine—even the name "Space Shuttle" implied the equivalent of a bus ride to the airport and carried the same expectations for reliability and economy. That sense of the routine built an operational culture within the shuttle working group that enabled and reinforced itself, and that had difficulty recognizing signals of anomalous events.

Yet anomalous events abounded. Though the O-rings had been troublesome from the earliest days of the shuttle's development, striking evidence came with the second flight, STS-2, in November of 1981. When the SRBs were disassembled for examination after the flight, the NASA engineers discovered that the combustion gas had indeed penetrated the putty and impinged on the O-ring. This was entirely contrary to the design expectations, which held that the gas would never reach the O-ring. Subsequent flights confirmed this deviance, and incremental attempts were made to address the problem. These fixes did not fully succeed, but the shuttle missions did. And so the working group culture came to accept a bit of char on an O-ring as normal. The original design expectations forgotten, compelling evidence could not be found to delay the launch of STS 51L. This is what Vaughan means by "the normalization of deviance." And so, the institutional framework exerts a powerful influence on what risks are acceptable and what risks are not (Vaughan 1996).

For our purpose in understanding the risk of new ventures, an important lesson emerges: that the culture and institutional norms of the innovator strongly influence the kinds of risk that are undertaken and their acceptability. This is true whether the innovating institution is large and complex like NASA or General Motors, or a garage startup with two partners and a dog. In Chapter 2, "Risk-Takers and Taking Risks," Drs. William B. Gartner and Jianwen Liao summarize their recent research into the risk-taking propensities of entrepreneurs. They conclude that those considered to be entrepreneurs are not inherently greater risk-takers than non-entrepreneurs. And successful entrepreneurs show no different risk propensities than the unsuccessful. To the contrary, Gartner and Liao show that the organizational and social context to be a principal influence on the risk of new ventures, and they suggest ways to manage it.

TOWARD IMPROVED DECISION-MAKING

Unlike physics, which is governed by laws that compel obedience, human behaviors are subject to central tendencies, and even these are inconsistently observed. Thus, neither of the chapters in Part I can offer a full prescription for the foibles of human nature. What they do, however, is provide a richer understanding of the cognitive biases that influence risk-taking, and in doing so, help to improve the likelihood of wise choice. Perhaps the best summary of advice for managing the risks of decision-making is to select decision-makers of known character and integrity, to seek a diversity of opinion in risky circumstances, and to carefully manage the risk and reward context within which the decisions are taken.

REFERENCES

Lansing, Alfred (1999) *Endurance: Shackleton's Incredible Voyage*. London: Weidenfeld & Nicolson.

Vaughan, Diane (1996) *The Challenger Launch Decision*. Chicago: University of Chicago Press.

Chapter 1

Managing an Entrepreneur's Risk-Taking Propensity

PHILIP BROMILEY, DEVAKI RAU, AND CARON H. ST. JOHN

We make investments in entrepreneurs—not businesses. Our fund would rather invest in a great entrepreneur and a mediocre business—than a mediocre entrepreneur with a great business concept.

We want entrepreneurs with experience—someone who has taken a business full circle from start-up to exit. Even if they have failed before, they will have learned from their mistakes. And, by trying again, they are demonstrating their toughness and resilience in the face of adversity.

We want entrepreneurs to have "skin in the game." We want them to have money and their livelihood at risk to show their commitment to the success of the business. We don't want them to be able to walk away if things get rough.

INVESTORS IN EARLY-STAGE entrepreneurial ventures often align with these beliefs—that the success of the business is more tied to the talent and insight of the entrepreneurial team than the business concept proposed in the prospectus; that experience accumulates and improves the likelihood of success with a second or third venture; and that by increasing the entrepreneur's up-front commitment to the venture—increasing their personal stake at risk—the business will benefit. How do these ideas mesh with what we know about risk and decision-making?

The word "entrepreneur" is derived from the French word "entreprendre" which means "to undertake." It is, by definition, action oriented. But, before taking action, the entrepreneur *decides* to take action, *decides* which actions to take, *decides* when to act and with what level of resource commitment. Once the new venture is launched, the entrepreneur and advisers decide the direction, timing, and investment for growth. If the venture is doing poorly, they decide what to do, including invest more or quit. These patterns of decisions made by entrepreneurs and their advisers largely determine the success or failure of the new venture over time. Ultimately everything that occurs in and around the formation and continuation of a new venture is a product of a decision made by a human mind, in an environment of uncertainty.

Economists and psychologists have studied decision-making and uncertainty for decades, with considerable attention in recent decades on the role of human cognition. *Human cognition* refers to the way we acquire, interpret, and use information, including the way we recognize opportunities, make decisions, and plan actions. These cognitive processes are influenced by a variety of personal and environmental factors, which is why two people who see the same factual information may draw very different conclusions about its meaning, why one person may see an opportunity that the other does not, why one person sees an action as risky that the other does not. Most importantly, psychologists and economists have learned that risk-taking propensity is not a permanent characteristic of an individual. A decision-maker's risk-taking propensity can change over time, differ by context, and be influenced by the presentation of the information about the circumstances. These studies of human cognition shed light on the entrepreneurial process and the risk-taking behavior often associated with entrepreneurs.

Venture investors have many formal ways of managing risk and reducing it to acceptable levels across their portfolio of investments. Our interest here is specific decisions made by entrepreneurs and investors involving uncertainty and risk—not the portfolio of investments. In this chapter, we focus first on how one influential theory of decision-making, prospect theory (Kahneman and Tversky 1979), can inform investors about the risk tendencies of entrepreneurs. Next, we provide an overview of other typical biases and problems in decision-making and the implications for risk management. We conclude with a brief discussion of how different personal values can influence decision-making over time—and the potential conflicts between investors and entrepreneurial teams.

DECISION-MAKING AND RISK: THE CONTRIBUTIONS OF PROSPECT THEORY

Prospect theory was developed by Daniel Kahneman and Amos Tversky in 1979. Kahneman and Tversky, both psychologists, were struggling with what appeared to be inconsistent findings in their efforts to apply expected utility theory from economics to the measurement of the risk-taking propensity of decision-makers. In some experiments, when presented with two choices with the same economic outcomes, decision-makers made different choices—sometimes risk-taking, sometimes risk-avoiding—suggesting something other than the theoretical predictions of expected utility theory were in play. The experiments suggested that decision-makers were influenced by the *framing* of the decision. If it was framed as a *gain* from their current situation, they preferred *certain* small gains over *uncertain* larger gains. So, for example, if a decision-maker were given a choice of receiving $100,000 with certainty or a 50 percent chance of $250,000 (expected value of $125,000 gain), the decision-maker would be likely to opt for the certain $100,000 gain. If, however, the choice was framed as a loss—a certain loss of $100,000 or a 50 percent chance of a $250,000 loss (expected value of loss, $125,000)—the decision-maker would consistently choose to chance the larger expected loss for the 50 percent chance of no loss at all.

This finding spoke loudly that decision-makers did not want to risk a sure thing if it was bettering their situation, but they were willing to gamble and risk a much larger loss if there was a possibility they could avoid the loss altogether. This asymmetric approach to decision-making—which was not mathematically logical following the precepts of expected utility theory—shed significant light on several biases that plague decision-makers, such as escalating commitment, inability to ignore sunk costs, the role of experience in forming rigid mental models, and, importantly, the role of reference points. As noted by Montier, in contrast to "expected utility theory, which predicts how decisions under uncertainty *should* be made, prospect theory is concerned with how decisions are *actually* made" (Montier 2002: 20). These researchers, who were eventually awarded the Nobel Prize for their ground-breaking work, demonstrated through experiments that choices are strongly influenced by the way the choice is framed, with the framing sometimes changing the decision in ways that we would not have predicted.

Framing and Reference Points

One of prospect theory's central ideas is the role of reference points in framing and influencing decision outcomes. Expectations and frames of reference influence our interpretations of information. For example, an investor would be disappointed by a venture that was supposed to earn $2 million but only earned $1 million, whereas if the venture were expected to earn $500,000 and instead earned $1 million, the investor would likely see that outcome as highly positive. Decision-makers view outcomes above the reference point as gains and outcomes below the reference point as losses.

With entrepreneurial ventures, reference points are often influenced by the successes and failures of other new ventures in the same sector—the stories that are told as well as the actual facts, if they are available. In forming reference points, decision-makers tend to under-weight outcomes with mid-range probabilities, but over-weight outcomes with extremely low probabilities. As described by Peter Bernstein (1998: 272), "we pay excessive attention to low-probability events accompanied by high drama and overlook events that happen in routine fashion." For example, most entrepreneurs and investors are well aware that most new ventures fail—that few survive and very few generate a substantial return. Entrepreneurs and investors talk about and remember the high profile successes and, even in the face of poor odds, believe they will be among the few to succeed. The successes are more salient—more

memorable, top-of-the-mind—and therefore more influential in subsequent referencing. Over time, these high profile successes and the drama that accompanies their
re-telling increase expectations and put upward pressure on reference points.

In addition to information about the context and circumstances of a decision,
reference points are influenced by the history and experience of the entrepreneurs
and investors who are involved. Work experience, education, industry affiliations,
professional associations, prior involvement in entrepreneurial activities, and recent
investment experience—all work together to reinforce mental models among investors
and entrepreneurs of "how things work." Investors and entrepreneurs who have experienced previous investment successes will draw on those successes in establishing
decision reference points for the next new venture. They are likely to set bolder, higher
expectations because of the reinforcement of the recent successes: faster entry, higher
revenue expectations, more aggressive market share expansion, and faster growth of
organization and infrastructure. Investors and entrepreneurs who have experienced
failures may be more cautious, set somewhat lower expectations, or opt out of
subsequent entrepreneurial activity altogether.

Reference Points and Risk-Taking Propensity

Reference points—whether bold or cautious—serve to frame the decisions that
follow by influencing the perception of risk as well as the risk-taking propensity of
decision-makers. According to prospect theory, as described by Tvede (1999: 94),
"We have an irrational tendency to be less willing to gamble with profits than with
losses." In general, decision-makers are more willing to take on risk to avoid losses
than to speculate on large gains. That is, in choosing between *losses* of roughly the
same expected value, individuals tend toward the more risky decision. So, given a
choice of losing $1 million for sure and a gamble with a 50 percent chance of losing
nothing and a 50 percent chance of losing $2 million, most would choose the gamble.
If the gamble goes in their favor, decision-makers avoid the loss. If the gamble does
not go in their favor, however, the loss is twice what it would have been. In contrast,
in choosing between positive outcomes or *gains* of roughly the same expected value,
decision-makers tend toward the least risky option. Given a choice between $1 million
for sure and a gamble with a 50 percent chance of nothing and a 50 percent chance
of $2 million or more, most decision-makers choose the $1 million for sure. *Decision-
makers take greater risks to avoid losses than to pursue gains.*

For entrepreneurs and their investors, the start-up and early growth stages of a
new venture are often plagued by uncertainty and concern about missing the
opportunity altogether, losing the investment, and embarrassing the founding team.
When entrepreneurs paint the picture for investors of what their new venture involves,
they often see it as something that is there for the taking, as long as they move
quickly enough with the right team, right funding, and right strategy. The entry
decision may be framed as a form of loss avoidance—a certain negative (*others will
take it from us . . . if we don't move now, we will lose out*) compared to an uncertain
positive outcome. The more confident the team is about the new venture's advantages

(e.g. intellectual property position), the more likely they are to use loss-framing in launch decisions.

An infusion of venture capital is likely to have an escalating influence on the loss-framing propensity of new ventures. Whereas it relieves immediate cash flow concerns that might have propelled risky short-run decision-making, it raises the stakes overall—putting more money at risk of being lost, which can increase the likelihood of loss-framing and thus increase the risk-taking propensity of decision-makers. Some investors choose to manage the risk-accelerating effect of a large capital infusion by adding cash in much smaller increments when certain milestones are met rather than making a large commitment up front.

The decision framing is likely to be very different for an established firm that is considering the same business opportunity. For an established firm, when considering whether to reinvest earnings into the established healthy business—or make a large investment in a wholly new business opportunity with an uncertain outcome—decision-makers within established firms are more likely to frame the decision as one of gain. In addition, they will often choose to make the investment in the core business with its more certain returns than invest in the more uncertain but potentially more successful new opportunity.

Relative Framing and Mental Accounting

In one of their experiments, Tversky and Kahneman (1981) observed that decision-makers tend to parse information about specific decisions in ways that alter reference points. For example, the same decision-makers who would drive 10 minutes to save $25 on a $50 printer cartridge would be unlikely to drive 10 minutes to save $25 on a $500 business suit. In both situations, a 10-minute drive results in a $25 saving. In these experiments, decision-makers used reference points within the context of the specific decision rather than a global reference point about the relationship between 10 minutes and $25. The decision-makers seem to take into consideration either the "relative" savings (50 percent savings on the cartridge versus 5 percent on the suit) or what the item is "worth"—with some reckoning that the lower priced printer cartridge was most aligned with its real value. From a managerial perspective, however, the decision-maker did not consider the global question of whether it was worth 10 minutes of time and gasoline to save $25 and, if so, whether it was worth 20 minutes to save $50. By parsing the two transactions and subjecting them to two different reference points defined by the local context only, the more global question of what was best overall was lost.

In another experiment, the researchers demonstrated another form of mental accounting and framing. Participants were presented with two scenarios similar to these:

(1) You are going to the theater. When you leave for the theater, you have two $100 bills in your wallet. When you arrive, you find that you have lost one of the $100 bills. Would you spend the remaining $100 to purchase a $100 theater ticket?

(2) You are going to the theater. When you leave for the theater, you have a $100 theater ticket and a $100 bill in your wallet. When you arrive at the theater, you find that you have lost the theater ticket. Would you spend the remaining $100 to purchase a replacement theater ticket?

Interestingly, in the first scenario, decision-makers are highly *likely* to spend the $100 on the theater ticket—but, in the second scenario, they are highly *unlikely* to purchase a replacement ticket. Objectively, the ticket cost $100 and either $100 or a ticket valued at $100 was lost. The arithmetic is the same in either scenario. But decision-makers seem to group the cost of the previously purchased ticket with the cost of a new ticket—and conclude that they do not want to pay $200 for a $100 theater ticket. This is a form of *mental accounting*—where the assignment or grouping of a cost influences the reference points and ultimately the decision that was made.

In addition to illustrating how context and circumstances influence the reference points used in making decisions, the examples also illustrate that decision-makers, including entrepreneurs and investors, "tend to consider decision problems one at a time, often isolating the current problem from other choices that may be pending, as well as from future opportunities to make similar decisions" (Kahneman and Lovallo 1993). Combining this with the idea that when individuals view problems in isolation, their willingness to take risks is approximately constant even for decisions that vary in size, suggests a tendency toward risk imbalance within individuals. Specifically, individuals will tend toward excessive risk aversion for small decisions, where they ignore the effects of aggregation (Kahneman and Lovallo 1993). For investors, it is important to be aware of the tendency of decision-makers, including entrepreneurs, to establish local, relative reference points in some cases and to group and accumulate them in other cases.

Risk-Taking and Venture Stages

All decision-making in the face of uncertainty involves some level of risk-taking. For investors, it is particularly important to understand how the context and circumstances of a particular venture frame decision reference points. And, importantly, as decisions are made and successes and failures realized, the context and circumstances of the venture change as well—which alters reference points along the way. An entrepreneur who seems to be a risk-taker at one point in time may not be a risk-taker at another point in time. Each of the typical stages in the formation and growth of a new venture involves circumstances that influence reference points and risk-taking.

Reference points and risk-taking at start-up. Individuals who launch new ventures choose between their current activities and the new venture. A person who views his or her current employment situation as undesirable would tend to frame the decision to launch a venture as a choice between two negative outcomes—maintaining the current negative work situation (as a certain outcome) versus launching a new venture, which may have a relatively high probability of failure but has some probability of success. By using the current negative situation as the reference point, this decision becomes one of loss avoidance which will stimulate riskier decision-making. Even if the new venture had a slightly lower expected value than the current situation, the risk (and inherent potential for some low probability but high value outcomes) may motivate a dissatisfied individual to launch a venture. On the other hand, someone with a solid, high income job would generally frame the decision as a comparison of certain income (a positive situation) versus a gamble for greater income that could result in loss or gain. In that kind of decision framework, decision-makers generally avoid risk unless the probability of failure is very low and the pay-off is very high. Therefore, very capable people who could be successful entrepreneurs are unlikely to leave good jobs to pursue a venture unless there is more certainty, such as a contract with a first large customer or an alliance with an established, well-positioned partner.

Whereas investors may diversify their personal risk by investing in several ventures or financial instruments, most entrepreneurs do not. They invest their time and effort into one new venture at a time and may mortgage their home and take on personal debt on behalf of the venture. Entrepreneurs and their teams therefore accept essentially greater risks than the investor. To the degree that entrepreneurs have more ''skin in the game'' and therefore more to lose, they are likely to frame decisions in terms of potential losses and to be more risk-seeking.

Reference points and risk-taking as time passes. Prospect theory has another direct implication for investors and entrepreneurs—it explains how reference points for decisions are very different when the new venture is doing poorly and when it is succeeding. In the early stages of a venture, it is likely entrepreneurs and investors will frame decisions around loss avoidance (known as loss-framing). This leads to risk-taking, as noted earlier. If the venture performs poorly, it is likely to escalate the loss-framing—which may lead to excessive risk-taking and larger actual losses.

On the other hand, over time and with success, reference points of entrepreneurs and investors will continue to change. Investments and strategic choices will increasingly be viewed as potential gains from the current positive situation, which may lead to less risk-taking. Over time and with success, entrepreneurial start-ups begin to make choices and investments that look a lot like older, more established competitors. Similarly, venture capital funds that start out making investments in early-stage ventures often migrate to lower risk, mezzanine-stage ventures once they achieve success in the riskier segment.

COGNITIVE BIASES AND RISK

Other forms of cognitive bias may influence entrepreneurs, investors, and their reference points, with consequences for risk-taking. One of the most common forms of bias is *anchoring*. Anchoring involves placing an inappropriate level of emphasis on information that may be unimportant in the decision-making process—and then unconsciously applying that information to the decision. This tendency can be illustrated by the following experiment. Suppose two large groups of individuals are asked to answer two questions, one requiring a yes-no response and the other requiring an answer or estimate. The first group is asked: Is the population of Japan *50* million? (Yes or No) What is the population of Japan? (Provide best estimate). The second group is asked a different version of the first question: Is the population of Japan *125* million? What is the population of Japan? The average population estimate for the group that was initially asked if the population was 50 million will be much lower than the average for the group that was asked if the population was 125 million. These differences exist irrespective of whether participants said yes or no to the first population question. This example illustrates the degree to which we are open to suggestion and, without realizing it, incorporate those suggestions, whether accurate or inaccurate, into our reference points.

For an entrepreneurial venture, this kind of anchoring can be quite common since so many decisions are made in an environment of uncertainty with so much input from advisers and investors from different industries and different companies. What may have been true with one biotech start-up may not be true with the next one—but the "lessons learned" offered by an adviser can be treated as facts. The past experience and knowledge gained become part of the "conventional wisdom"—what entrepreneurs and investors think they know about the industry, the size of the opportunity, the likely response or strategy of competitors, what customers value most in the purchase decision, the relationship between scale and costs, or the price ceiling or floor. On the one hand, it can be the tacit knowledge that is true, but that is unarticulated and taken for granted. On the other hand, it can be quite wrong and since it is not understood to be built on assumptions, it influences decisions but is never questioned or tested. Anchoring of this type can increase risk by distorting decisions and is best managed by being careful to call-out the assumptions underlying any estimates, forecasts, or decisions—and by planning to test or evaluate them.

Another form of cognitive bias that is quite common in the venture community is the *bandwagon effect*. This involves the tendency to believe things because other reputable people believe them and to follow the actions of credible leaders in the community. As with anchoring bias, this is another example of taking information— accurate or inaccurate—for granted and not questioning its validity or its applicability to the uniqueness of the new circumstance. To some degree, bandwagoning is at work when customers converge on a common set of standards and when a dominant design emerges in an industry. In those instances, following the lead of others may pay off. But bandwagoning is also at work when new ventures imitate the approaches of successful firms that went before them, only to find that circumstances and context have changed and those approaches no longer work. Bandwagoning is also at work when a few high profile successes in a particular technology sector lead investors to rush to get in on a game they don't completely understand, causing over-investment in marginal business models (as was the case with the dot-com bust). As with anchoring, the key to resisting bandwagon effects is to state and test assumptions that underlie uncertain strategic and financial decisions.

Confirmation bias and the *endowment effect* are two forms of decision-making bias that arise from an inward focus. Confirmation bias refers to a tendency to interpret information in a way that confirms previously held beliefs and ideas and to disregard information that might provide contradictory evidence. Many entrepreneurs suffer from confirmation bias in that they focus exclusively on the information that confirms the existence of the opportunity they want to pursue and their approach. They may "trust their gut" and rely on "hunches"—and then see only the evidence that supports these preconceived ideas. Any advisers or colleagues who question the opportunity or provide contradictory evidence may be condemned as nay-sayers. The conventional wisdom in the entrepreneurial community is that it is common for others to not see what the entrepreneur can see. Investors who have been successful entrepreneurs themselves have the most credibility in these situations and can use their influence to temper risky behavior even when evidence and facts are not enough.

Entrepreneurs often succumb to the endowment effect when negotiating investment deals and partnership arrangements with other companies. They place a higher value on what they are selling than they would be willing to pay for the same thing, if positions were reversed. They demand much more to give up something than they would be willing to pay to have it (Kahneman et al. 1991). This conflict can result in difficulty taking on investors, negotiating financing arrangements, and forming strategic alliances. It is best managed by bringing in independent third parties to manage perceptions and negotiate agreements.

Escalating commitment or irrational escalation refers to the tendency to justify incremental increases in commitment to a decision or investment in the business based on what has happened in the past, even though new evidence suggests otherwise. This is sometimes referred to as the sunk-cost problem and relates to the difficulty of letting go emotionally of money that is already gone. This is particularly problematic in ventures where large upfront investments must be made to mature technology and conduct expensive customer trials. The fear of losing all of the investment made thus far is a classic example of loss-framing that can lead to risky gambles to avoid the loss. Investors and entrepreneurs are equally likely to be drawn into this form of bias because they share concerns about the financial investment. Independent third parties, such as external board members with no financial stake, can be an objective source of information and balance in these situations.

ENTREPRENEURS AND INVESTORS: SHARED VALUES

One of the most common issues that bedevils investor–entrepreneur relations, however, arises not from cognitive bias and its implications for risk-taking. It is the different values and goals that investors and entrepreneurial management teams bring to the launch of a new venture. Entrepreneurs have personal goals and expectations, which are influenced by their own history, experiences, and circumstances. Similarly, investors have their own personal goals and expectations that reflect their history and experiences. When entrepreneurs and investors form a new venture, they bring to the venture personal values such as wealth attainment, autonomy, freedom to innovate, control, and others. Entrepreneurs will place a high value on financial returns, but they are also very likely to be interested in autonomy, control, and recognition for creating an impactful new business. Entrepreneurs often resist the efforts of investors to move the business toward a quick exit or take actions that dilute the entrepreneur's ownership stake. Venture investors bring their own values to the venture as well. Like entrepreneurs, they too may value wealth attainment, control, autonomy, or leisure, but primarily for themselves, not for the entrepreneur and management team. In addition, investors may have their own beliefs about the probability of the entrepreneurial team achieving success within a time horizon that the investor considers reasonable. Investors and entrepreneurs may conflict over a mismatch of values and beliefs, and the resulting interpretation of goals and outcomes.

In some cases, the differences in personal goals can result in different reference points for specific decisions such as the ones discussed throughout this chapter. An entrepreneur may focus on growth and market share gains and sacrifice profits because of a belief that competitors will challenge the market position. In that same situation, investors may choose to focus on more careful growth that balances market share with profit-taking. For the investors, failing to meet profit goals is a negative — but for the entrepreneur, profit-taking was deliberately subordinated to the revenue growth goal for reasons the entrepreneur believed were strategic.

A recent front page article in the *Wall Street Journal*, "Facebook CEO in No Rush to 'Friend' Wall Street" (Vascellaro 2010) illustrates the potential conflict between the values of entrepreneurs and investors. Most analysts on Wall Street agree that taking Facebook public would make Mark Zuckerberg, the CEO, the world's richest 20-something. Zuckerberg, however, seems to value autonomy and control over wealth. He realizes that if Facebook goes public, he will face pressure to meet Wall Street financial expectations rather than pursuing his own strategic agenda for the company. Rather than move toward an IPO, he struck a deal with an investor to buy the stock of employees who wanted an exit event, without a meaningful dilution of his own stake — all against the advice of other, more experienced investors.

Although most investors and entrepreneurs would argue that they have conversations about exit strategies, financial goals, and controlling interests very early on in the investment negotiation process, time and success have a way of changing those agreed-upon decisions as well as everyone's memory of them. As discussed in this chapter, reference points are influenced by the changing context and circumstances. A young, inexperienced entrepreneur who is willing to listen to experienced investors gains confidence with success and may begin to challenge the advice of those mentors. A serial entrepreneur who regrets exiting a first venture early may choose to hang on longer the second time with expectations of even higher financial returns. With larger investments at risk, fear of failure can cause some entrepreneurs to take risks they would never have considered early in the life of the venture.

FINAL THOUGHTS

If one has to jump a stream and knows how wide it is, he will not jump. If he doesn't know how wide it is, he'll jump and six times out of ten he'll make it.

Persian Proverb

As a society, whether we admit it or not, we want our entrepreneurs to be risk-takers. As described in the proverb above, we want them to exhibit confidence in the face of uncertainty rather than timidity when peering into the unknown. Interestingly, the preferred terms required by serious investors serve to exacerbate the risk-taking propensity of entrepreneurs. Entrepreneurs are asked to place all-or-nothing bets on the success of the venture—with "skin in the game" and the inability to walk away. With their livelihoods and reputations at stake, they are likely to frame decisions in terms of loss which, as we discussed in this chapter, will lead to riskier decisions. Serial, successful entrepreneurs, those preferred by investors, are likely to expect bigger and better outcomes for their next venture, pushing decision reference points upward and creating an environment for more aggressive, riskier decisions. Large infusions of investment capital that give investors an influential stake can increase risk-taking—because there is more to lose.

When coupled with the cognitive biases that are typical in all decision-making and the pronounced uncertainty of the new venture context, it is likely that these risks will be taken without full and accurate information. The proverb at the beginning of this section notes boldness in the face of uncertainty. Ironically, it also queues up another idea about salience and bias in decision-making. The next entrepreneur to approach the stream will likely know the stories of the entrepreneurs who jumped the stream successfully but will know nothing of the ones who chose not to jump or failed in the effort. The entrepreneur will not know how wide the stream is—how likely he or she is to succeed under the specific capabilities and circumstances—but, "if others did it, so can I."

As we've discussed, investors can play a role in managing entrepreneurs' changing reference points, biases, and risk-taking propensity. Venture investors themselves can provide the entrepreneur and the management team with an outside, more balanced perspective. By being aware of the forms of cognitive bias and the relationship between reference points, framing and risk, investors are more equipped to counterbalance these effects. Furthermore, the risk propensity and biases of entrepreneurs and investors can be counterbalanced by advisers who bring different frames of reference to the decisions at hand. For example, objective insights can be developed from independent entrepreneurs who have successfully navigated in similar situations, independent advisers and board members who do not have a financial stake in the company, and consultants with deep experience in the technologies or markets of interest. Investors can challenge entrepreneurs to dig deeper—to surface the tacit knowledge that can be the foundation for inaccurate assumptions and biased decision-making. Investors can help entrepreneurs to consciously frame decisions in a more positive light—to force a comparison of the decisions that would be made if framed as a gain and as a loss. For example, investors can encourage their entrepreneurs to contrast the possible outcomes of different strategies and approaches, and to explicitly consider alternatives that would reduce risk, or even add to it.

Finally, investors can assess the values and experiences of entrepreneurs to get a glimpse of the mental model that will be brought to the decision process. To manage cognitive bias and ill-advised risk-taking, investors should seek an entrepreneur who is willing to be coached, seeks contradictory input, is confident admitting what he or she doesn't know, and is able to step away from problems and decisions to observe them from different reference points. Both fear of failure and rash overconfidence are likely to be recipes for excess risk-taking.

REFERENCES

Bernstein, P. L. (1998) *Against the Gods: The Remarkable Story of Risk*. New York: John Wiley & Sons.

Kahneman, D. and Lovallo, D. (1993) "Timid Choices and Bold Forecasts: A Cognitive Perspective on Risk Taking," *Management Science*, 39 (1): 17–31.

Kahneman, D. and Tversky, A. (1979) "Prospect Theory: An Analysis of Decision under Risk," *Econometrica*, 47 (2): 263–291.

Kahneman, Daniel, Knetsch, Jack L., and Thaler, Richard H. (1991) "Anomalies: The Endowment Effect, Loss Aversion, and Status Quo Bias," *The Journal of Economic Perspectives* (American Economic Association), 5 (1): 193–206.

Montier, James (2002) *Darwin's Mind: The Evolutionary Foundations of Heuristics and Biases*. Dresdner KleinwortWasserstein – Global Equity Strategy.

Tvede, Lars (1999) *The Psychology of Finance*. Chichester: Wiley. First edition published by Norwegian University Press in hardcover in 1990.

Tversky, A. and Kahneman, D. (1981) "The Framing of Decisions and the Psychology of Choice," *Science*, 211 (4481): 453–458.

Vascellaro, J. E. (2010) "Facebook CEO in No Rush to 'Friend' Wall Street," *Wall Street Journal*, CCLV (31): A1.

Chapter 2

Risk-Takers and Taking Risks

WILLIAM B. GARTNER AND
JIANWEN LIAO

INTRODUCTION

THE CONUNDRUM OF ENTREPRENEURIAL risk-taking reminds us of a conversation we have had with a number of CEOs. The owner/founder of a very successful innovative business calls with this question:

"How can I make my employees more entrepreneurial? As the business has grown, they simply don't want to take any risks to pursue new opportunities. What can I do?"

"How do you reward failure?"

"What do you mean? Reward failure?"

"Well, let's take this simplistic view of how venture capitalists think about failure and success when they invest in new opportunities. Venture capitalists never just invest in one deal: they try to spread their chances of having a success by investing in many different businesses. So, let's say that a venture capitalist has invested in ten opportunities. What do you think are the chances of any one of those ten opportunities becoming a success? Well, the rule of thumb is that five of those ten opportunities will simply fail, and the venture capitalist will lose whatever money has been invested. And, three of those opportunities will become businesses that are not successful enough for the venture capitalist either to cash out, sell to another company, or take public. These three would be called 'the living dead': the businesses are alive, but they will never provide a return to the venture capitalist. So, that leaves, in all likelihood, two businesses that will be the ones that generate a sufficient return to make up for all of the losses incurred from the other eight 'failed' businesses."

"And your point is?"

> "Investing in entrepreneurial ventures is mostly about investing in failures. A venture capitalist gets to look at hundreds of opportunities that might result in a high potential venture, and, even after they select the ten best from these hundreds, venture capitalists still end up with only two of those ten that succeed. So, if you invested in the ten best opportunities that your employees championed in your company, what will you do with the employees that are likely to fail in eight of those efforts?"
>
> "Fire them. I only want to support the two efforts that succeed."
>
> "And, firing your 'failures' will motivate your employees to take more risks?"

In entrepreneurship and innovation you can't, before the race, pick the winners. If venture capitalists could know, beforehand, which ventures were going to be successful, then they wouldn't make eight out of ten choices that lead to failure. In entrepreneurship, choosing failures is a part of the process of having successes.

So, since failing is more likely than success for high potential ventures, does it mean that the entrepreneurs involved in those ventures are taking larger risks than those individuals who choose jobs? No. What gets muddled is the discrepancy between "risk-takers" and "taking risks." A "risk-taker" is a type of person, while "taking risks" is a behavior. We all take risks, but not all of us are risk-takers. Parsing the differences between "risk-takers" and "taking risks" is the primary focus of this chapter.

For this discussion, risk-taking will be defined as the willingness to take action based on the perception of possible future gains or losses. An individual with a propensity for high levels of risk, that is, a "risk-taker," would be willing to accept high levels of variability in the gains or losses of future choices. A low risk-taking propensity would signal a willingness to accept low levels of variability in the gains or losses of future choices. An example of the difference between high and low variability in gains or losses: high variability might be taking a chance to earn either one million dollars or zero dollars; and low variability might be taking a chance to earn either $600,000 or $400,000. Both decisions have the same average outcome: $500,000. Yet the choice of one million dollars or zero dollars would be perceived as more risky: the variation in the outcomes is greater.

Are entrepreneurs "risk-takers?" That is, are they more prone to engage in actions that are perceived as having higher levels of risk than *others*? We highlight *others* because one of the important issues in exploring risk involves identifying the kinds of individuals that represent "entrepreneurs" compared to the kinds of individuals that represent "non-entrepreneurs." As will be discussed later in this chapter, determining what constitutes "entrepreneurs" as a group, compared to what constitutes "non-entrepreneurs" as a group, is problematic. Be that as it may, this chapter will suggest that entrepreneurs are, in general, no more likely to seek higher levels of risk compared to *others*. Entrepreneurs are not "risk-takers" per se, as much as they, like all of us, take risks, and the variation and magnitude of the risks that entrepreneurs take, in general, are not significantly different from the risks we are all, in general, willing to assume.

The chapter is structured as follows: we offer insights about the tendency to believe that entrepreneurs are "risk-takers" and therefore more willing to accept higher levels of risk than others. Previous research on entrepreneurial risk-taking is reviewed to show how this belief that entrepreneurs are risk-takers is pervasive, even when there is substantial evidence to the contrary. We argue that the likelihood that entrepreneurs will take risks is primarily influenced by the context of risk-taking, rather than the personality characteristics of risk-takers themselves. The chapter concludes with some insights into a very simple framework to view the contexts that determine the kinds of risks that individuals are willing to take when they engage in entrepreneurial activities. Based on this framework, we provide some suggestions for enhancing or reducing entrepreneurial risk-taking behaviors.

VARIATION IN ENTREPRENEURSHIP

It is important to recognize that the context for entrepreneurship and innovation has a significant influence on how and why individuals go about these processes (Gartner 2008). As described in the Introduction to this book, the processes of innovation and entrepreneurship are affected by a variety of forces beyond the actions and motivations of the entrepreneurs and innovators who initiate these endeavors. The kinds of environments, the types of businesses, the specific modes of innovation and entrepreneurial activity: all influence, and are influenced by, the kinds of individuals engaged in entrepreneurship and innovation (Gartner 1985).

If the variety of entrepreneurial situations is so broad (i.e. there are many different entrepreneurial environments, entrepreneurial firms, entrepreneurial processes) it should stand to reason that there should also be a very large variety of different kinds of individuals engaged in entrepreneurship (Gartner 1988). We hope that this illustration will suffice for demonstrating variation in entrepreneurship and entrepreneurs.

Inc Magazine (www.inc.com) publishes a yearly survey of the 5,000 fastest-growing companies (measured by change in gross sales, revenue, and employees over a three-year period) in the United States. While one might assume that most high growth companies are primarily in high technology industries, the list of 5,000 firms is divided into 26 different industry groups: from advertising to travel. None of the 26 industry groups accounts for a significant percentage of the total.

It would be unlikely that all of the business models for these 26 different industry groups (to name a few more: construction, education, energy, financial services, health, insurance, security) would be the same. In addition, it would be unlikely that the business models within a particular industry would all be the same. For example, in the food and beverage category, the fastest-growing firm, MonaVie, which grew from $14.3 million in 2005 to $854.9 million in 2008 (a 5,833.0 percent growth rate) sells nutritional supplements and products based on the Brazilian acai berry through person-to-person sales. The next highest growth company in this category is GourmetGiftBaskets.com, which grew from $253,000 in 2005 to $8.5 million in 2008 (a 3,260.5 percent growth rate). GourmetGiftBaskets.com sells food and beverage gift baskets to online customers. Each company has a very different business model (multi-level marketing versus business-to-consumer ecommerce) compared to the other.

So, if the types of competitive environments for high growth firms vary, if the businesses and business models for these high growth firms vary, then why wouldn't the kinds of individuals who start and operate these many different kinds of businesses be different as well? To assume that individuals in this wide array of industries and businesses are taking the same kinds of risks, or would have the same risk propensity, would be a stretch of imagination. So, why is there this tendency to believe that entrepreneurs are risk-takers?

THE FUNDAMENTAL ATTRIBUTION ERROR

One of the primary tenets of social psychology is based on the observation that all people will make attributions (inferences) about the causes of other people's behaviors (Heider 1958). There are, broadly, two types of attributions that we offer for explaining other people's actions: internal attributions or external attributions. Internal attributions ascribe the causes of behavior to the disposition of the individual. External attributions ascribe the causes of behavior to the situation. For example, a quick perusal of information (books, academic articles, websites) about reasons for business failure will show that the majority of reasons that outside observers (such as lawyers, lenders, consultants, government policy-makers, etc.) will ascribe for why businesses fail is due to the person who owned the business (e.g. poor manager, poor planner, poor sales person, lazy, etc.). This is an internal attribution: the failure of the business is attributed to the business owner. Yet, when asking the owner/managers of failed businesses for reasons for their business failure, most of these entrepreneurs will offer external causes for their demise (e.g. government regulation, the recession, change in consumer tastes, etc.). Regardless of which of the two views might be accurate, this tendency for observers to assume that other people's behaviors are driven by internal factors, rather than by factors in their situation, is labeled the fundamental attribution error (Jones and Harris 1967; Ross 1977).

In the case of "risk-taking," then, the fundamental attribution error is to attribute the "taking risks" that we observe individuals engaged in as a characteristic of the individuals involved, rather than to view the "taking risks" as an aspect of the situation. Taking risks does not mean that the individual is a "risk-taker," that is, the behaviors that we see as "risk-taking" should not imply that these behaviors are caused by the person's risk-taking disposition. That is the fundamental attribution error: to believe that all behaviors are caused by the motivations of the individual. We assume that "risk-takers" take risks, and therefore, "risk-takers" have a need to take risks. More specific to entrepreneurial risks: we see individuals engage in activities to start a business; we assume that these activities are risky (i.e. compared to our experience of working at a job, which for most of us seems to be a more secure activity); and then we assume that these individuals have a higher need to take risks than us. Yet, the risk-taking that we observe individuals engaged in may not, from the perspective of the individuals engaged in those behaviors, be viewed as risky at all. An example: John Morris, an entrepreneur in Seattle, Washington who has successfully started a number of businesses in food manufacturing and food distribution tells his entrepreneurship story as one of risk avoidance:

> I became an entrepreneur because, if I had a job, I would have one person determining my success or failure: my boss. That seems risky to me. By having my own business, I would have lots of different bosses, my customers, who are the ones who determine my success or failure. With so many bosses, I limit my risk. I can be sure to please some of them, and, I can look for others to please if some are unhappy.
>
> (Morse 1992)

Academics, who study entrepreneurial risk-taking, have tended to get stuck in the fundamental attribution error. Prior scholarship on risk-taking reflects this confusion by attributing the behaviors of starting businesses as risky, and then ascribing these risky behaviors as caused by the internal dispositions of those individuals engaged in those behaviors: entrepreneurs start businesses → we view the process of starting a business as "risky" → entrepreneurs are therefore taking risks → entrepreneurs are risk-takers. Ironically, there is little substantive academic evidence that entrepreneurs are "risk-takers."

A BRIEF REVIEW OF ENTREPRENEURSHIP SCHOLARSHIP ON RISK-TAKING

The idea of risk-taking is in the genesis of conceptions about entrepreneurship. One of the first individuals to use the term "entrepreneur," Richard Cantillon (1755/ 2001), viewed the process of entrepreneurship as that of undertaking the risks inherent in buying and selling in the marketplace where prices were uncertain. The individuals who were willing to bear this marketplace uncertainty were also the ones who would reap the benefits (or losses) from this risk-taking. Say (1880/1971) espoused a similar view: entrepreneurs were individuals who were willing to accept the risks involved with assembling the resources required to produce goods that would be sold in the marketplace. Those surpluses of funds gained from sales over costs were labeled as entrepreneurial rents that accrued to these entrepreneurs. Frank Knight (1921), who first made the distinction between risk (the probabilities of future outcomes are known) and uncertainty (the probabilities of future outcomes are not known), saw the entrepreneur as willing to assume uncertainty for the likelihood of future profit. So, if entrepreneurs take risks, are they also "risk-takers?"

It wasn't until 1980 that Robert Brockhaus (1980) undertook a systematic study to determine whether entrepreneurs were, in fact, "risk-takers": different from other individuals in their willingness to take risks. An important aspect of Brockhaus' study involved the way he went about selecting individuals to represent a group of entre-preneurs and a comparison group of non-entrepreneurs. In his study entrepreneurs were individuals who had quit their jobs within the last three months and had started an ongoing business. The non-entrepreneurs were composed of two types of indi-viduals: those who had quit their jobs within the last three months and were currently working for another organization, and those who had changed positions within their organizations within the last three months. All individuals involved in this study, therefore, had undertaken a change in their jobs within the past three months.

All participants in the Brockhaus study were asked to fill out the Choice Dilemmas Questionnaire—CDQ (Wallach and Kogan 1959: 1961). This questionnaire presents 12 situations where individuals make judgments about the probability of success that would be sufficient for them to assume the risk of a particular choice. For example, a scenario might describe an individual who had a secure job who was contemplating starting a business that would pay significantly more than the current position. Respondents would select a success probability (e.g. "the chances are 1 in 10 that the company will be financially sound," to "the chances are 9 in 10 that the company will be financially sound," to "Mr. A should not take the job no matter what the probability") for taking the risk of starting the business. Scores on this questionnaire can range from 12 to 120, with a lower score indicating a higher propensity to take risks.

The average scores and standard deviations on the CDQ for the three groups in the Brockhaus study were essentially the same. There were no differences in the risk-taking propensities of entrepreneurs compared to other individuals who had also undertaken a job change in the past three months. Indeed, when Brockhaus compared the scores of the entrepreneurs to the scores that Kogan and Wallach (1964) had generated on a sample of the general population, they were essentially the same. The empirical evidence runs counter to the sense that individuals who appear to be taking risks are risk-takers.

There have been two concerns with Brockhaus' study: (1) the sample was small, there were 31 individuals in each group, 93 total individuals for the entire study, and (2) many scholars felt the CDQ instrument provided a flawed measure of risk. In the ensuing years, numerous studies have been undertaken to replicate Brockhaus' findings and improve on his research process by using larger samples and better measures of risk.

Yet, the culmination of over 30 years of research on entrepreneurial risk-taking has led to few, if any, conclusive insights. For example, the two major meta-analyses of research studies comparing risk-taking propensities of entrepreneurs to others generated conflicting findings. In the first meta-analysis, Stewart and Roth (2001) analyzed 12 studies that used, primarily, the risk-taking scale in the Jackson Person-ality Inventory (Jackson 1976). Their findings indicated that entrepreneurs who were "growth-oriented founders" were more likely to have higher levels of risk-taking propensity than "income-oriented" entrepreneurs, who were more likely to have higher levels of risk-taking propensity than managers. In contrast, Miner and Raju (2004) analyzed 14 studies that primarily used the Risk Avoidance subscale of the Miner Sentence Completion Scale—Form T (Miner 1986), a projective measure of risk-proneness, and they found that entrepreneurs were less likely to be prone to taking risks compared to managers.

Meta-analyses of the combination of all of the studies in Stewart and Roth (2001) and Miner and Raju (2004) produced conflicting findings. One study suggested that entrepreneurs and managers had similar risk propensities (Miner and Raju 2004), while another re-analysis (Stewart and Roth 2004) suggested that entrepreneurs had higher risk propensities than managers. The authors of these opposing views posit the reasons for the differences in the results for analyses of the same studies were due to the selection of specific studies to include that reliably measure risk propensity and represent "valid" samples of entrepreneurs. Neither side could agree on which specific studies of risk-taking propensity should be the correct ones to include for analyses. So, combining different studies produced different results.

At a more fundamental level, these meta-analyses of various studies are problematical because of how individuals are defined as either "entrepreneurs" or "managers." The samples of "entrepreneurs" used for studies of risk-taking propensity typically include founders of businesses that started their companies long ago. Therefore, one must assume that an individual's propensity for risk did not change over time, so that the risk-taking propensity score that an individual had as a founder would be similar to the risk-taking propensity score that the individual had later as the owner of an ongoing firm. Rarely did any of the studies control for the length of time between when the founder started the business and when the founder participated in the risk propensity survey. The time between these events could be years or decades. In addition, these studies provided few details about the characteristics of the "managers" used to compare to the entrepreneurs. Were these mid-level managers? Did these managers have profit and loss responsibilities? Could these managers make decisions to expand their divisions to pursue new opportunities? Could these managers personally profit from the upside of their decisions, and were these managers likely to be punished if their actions resulted in failures? In what ways, then, were these "managers" in these various samples similar or different to the entrepreneurs they were compared with? Surprisingly, we could not find evidence, over the past 30 years, of any studies that replicated Brockhaus' sampling strategy of finding individuals who had just started new businesses with a comparison group of managers who had just started new jobs.

The fundamental attribution error, then, in these risk-taking studies is to assume the risk-taking is due to the characteristics of the individual rather than to explore whether risk-taking was also influenced by the situation. Since none of these studies (except for Brockhaus 1980) controlled for characteristics of the situation, we are left with research that assumes, by default, that risk-taking is about risk-takers. By focusing only on the risk-taking propensity of these individuals, then, prior research did not assess whether the situations of the respondents might have influenced their choices.

RECENT RESEARCH ON ENTREPRENEURIAL RISK-TAKING

There are two recent research efforts that have sought to study individuals in the actual process of starting businesses (which are described below) that have explored their risk profiles. Assuming that one would want to look at the risk-taking perceptions of entrepreneurs while they were actually in the process of starting businesses (thereby having an opportunity to control for characteristics of their situation), such research samples would solve many of the problems of samples biased toward studying entrepreneurs long after their startup efforts. Such a longitudinal sample of individuals in the process of starting businesses exists: the Panel Study of Entrepreneurial Dynamics (PSED) (Gartner et al. 2004). The PSED is a longitudinal dataset of individuals in the process of starting businesses who were identified from a random digit dialing telephone survey of 64,622 adults in the United States (Reynolds and Curtin 2004). The nascent entrepreneurs in the sample were followed for five years after their initial interview to ascertain whether these individuals were successful at starting their businesses. For comparative purposes, the dataset also contains a generalizable random sample of individuals in the general population.

In the first study (Xu and Ruef 2004), the risk perceptions of nascent entrepreneurs were compared to the generalizable sample of individuals in the general population. They theorized two forms of risk tolerance that may lead individuals toward entrepreneurial activities: strategic and non-strategic (we will use the word "generic" instead of non-strategic). Strategic risks focus on the perceptions of specific risks associated with the development of a new business while generic risks focus on the perceptions of risks associated with situations endemic to all individuals (e.g. perceptions of the likelihood that a new business, in general, will succeed; estimates of the size that new businesses, in general, might grow to in five years).

Specifically, for *strategic risk-taking propensity*, nascent entrepreneurs were asked about their preferences among three ventures which have the same expected payout—the probability of success times the profit (PSED question QH1). The three options were: a profit of $5,000,000 with a 20 percent chance of success; a profit of $2,000,000 with a 50 percent chance of success; and a profit of $1,250,000 with an 80 percent chance of success. These three options were subsequently coded as 3, 2 and 1 respectively. For *generic risk-taking behavior*, nascent entrepreneurs were asked two related questions. The first question asked: "Considering all the new businesses that will be started in the U.S. this year, what percentage do you expect to close within five years? (PSED question QN1)" The second question asks: "Of all new business starts, what percent will eventually be worth $0 to 499,999, $500,000 to 999,999, $1,000,000 to 4,999,999, $5,000,000 to 9,999,999, and $10,000,000 or more, respectively? (PSED questions QN2a–QN2e)." The expected entrepreneurial profit would be calculated by summing the cross product of the median of each category and the estimated corresponding percentage, multiplied by the probability of success (which equals 1 subtracting the probability of failure rate estimated in the first question). The measures were standardized in $1,000s for subsequent analysis.

Xu and Ruef (2004) found that nascent entrepreneurs were more risk-adverse than the sample representing the U.S. population for both strategic and generic risks. More specifically, they found that entrepreneurs were less likely to select business opportunities that had higher variations in potential outcomes compared to the comparison sample. And they found that nascent entrepreneurs were more likely to estimate that new businesses had higher chances of failing and, if started, would have lower levels of growth, compared to the responses of the comparison sample. Based on these findings, then, individuals involved in the process of starting businesses, in general, are not "risk-takers" any more than the population as a whole.

As an extension of the Xu and Ruef (2004) study, Gartner and Liao (in press) explored whether the risk-taking propensity (strategic and generic) of these nascent entrepreneurs had any effect on the likelihood of actually starting businesses. The risk-taking propensity of individuals who actually start businesses could be different than the risk-taking propensity of individuals who gave up, or are still trying to start new ventures. The successful entrepreneurs could be the individuals with higher risk propensities than the failures. In addition, we explored how a nascent entrepreneur's strategic and generic risk-taking propensity might be influenced by views of environmental uncertainty and aspirations for venture growth, and whether these constructs (risk, uncertainty, and aspirations) affect the likelihood that a nascent entrepreneur will succeed at starting an ongoing business. The measure of uncertainty taps into perceptions of the situation each entrepreneur faced. In addition, the aspiration measure taps into the entrepreneur's desire to pursue larger or smaller opportunities.

To ascertain perceptions of *environmental uncertainty* (QD1a–QD1k), we used an 11-item measure from a PSED mailing survey (Matthew and Human 2004). These items are related to nascent entrepreneurs' perceptions of their ability to understand or to predict the state of various environmental conditions due to lack of information or uncertainty about that environment. A factor analysis of the 11 items generated three interpretable factors: financial uncertainty, competitive uncertainty, and operational uncertainty, which have Cronbach Alphas of 7.1, 6.3, and 6.1, respectively. Due to the low reliability of the competitive and operational uncertainty scores, and also considering the very early stage of venture formation, we chose financial uncertainty as a key uncertainty measure and a composite score of these measures was also created for subsequent analysis.

Growth aspiration was measured by the question: "Describe your preference for the future size of this business: 1) I want the business to be as large as possible, or 2) I want a size I can manage myself or with a few key employees?" The first option is coded as "2" and the second option is coded as "1."

The findings from our analyses indicated that an entrepreneur's risk propensity had no relationship to the likelihood of successfully starting a business. In other words, whether an entrepreneur has a high or low propensity for risk (either strategic or generic), the likelihood of successfully starting a business is not affected. Entrepreneurs with high scores (i.e. the risk-takers) are no more likely to start a business than the risk-averse. In addition, the moderating variables—growth aspirations and perceptions of uncertainty—while correlated to generic risk (nascent entrepreneurs who sought higher levels of growth and/or perceived high levels of uncertainty were more likely to score higher on the generic risk measure, only) did not correlate significantly to success at creating a new venture. The findings from these two studies suggest that perceptions of risk do not differentiate between entrepreneurs and others, or between successful and unsuccessful entrepreneurs.

Perceptions of risk, then, are simply not a meaningful way to grasp the nature of the entrepreneur.

Now, this is not to say that there is no variation in the risk profiles of entrepreneurs, overall, or of the general population, overall. Some entrepreneurs do have higher propensities for strategic and generic risk compared to others. Some individuals in the general population have higher propensities for strategic and generic risk compared to others. What our results do indicate is that, in general, for entrepreneurs as a group, their scores on the strategic and generic risk propensity measures are not statistically different from scores from the sample of the general population. In addition, the risk scores of entrepreneurs don't seem to affect the likelihood that they will successfully start a firm.

So, to assume that an individual's risk-taking propensity has some relationship to whether they will be more likely to act entrepreneurially, or be more likely to succeed as an entrepreneur, is, therefore, the fundamental attribution error. Engaging in entrepreneurship does not, inherently, stem from a personal characteristic such as "risk-taking." While entrepreneurs do take risks, they are not more likely to be "risk-takers" than anyone else. So, if entrepreneurs are not "risk-takers," any more than others in the population, how might we view taking risks in entrepreneurial situations?

WHO WINS OR LOSES? A FRAMEWORK FOR EVALUATING TAKING ENTREPRENEURIAL RISKS

We have found a very insightful framework for helping individuals distinguish between the kinds of situations that are likely to (or not) promote entrepreneurial risk-taking (Cipolla 1987). The framework is based on this assumption: our lives are a series of transactions between other people. These transactions occur whenever a person is involved with another person and represent experiences where there can be gains or losses between the two parties. When person A initiates an activity with person B, there is an effect on both A and B. We can diagram the outcomes of these transactions as a two-by-two matrix that shows the relative gain or loss between A and B (see Figure 2.1).

We label activities where both A and B win based on A's efforts, as *entrepreneuring* (the word is taken from Steyaert (2007)) (see Quadrant E in Figure 2.1). Entrepreneuring is creating situations where both parties to the interaction will likely gain. When entrepreneurs sell products or provide services, ideally the buyers of these products/services are better off because the transaction fills a need. These entrepreneurs are also better off because they make money through the transaction.

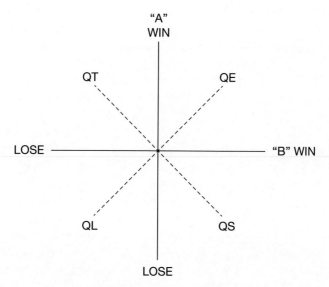

Figure 2.1. Interaction Gains and Losses

This also applies to interactions in organizations. We want individuals to initiate projects where they win (i.e. promotions, bonuses, awards, etc.) and the organization benefits (i.e. increased sales, growth in earnings, higher levels of productivity) as well from these innovations and entrepreneurial activities. Yet, not all situations are "win-win."

In the "lose-win" quadrant (Quadrant S), a person who initiates an activity where he or she loses and the other person wins *sacrifices*: Person A's actions result in a situation where A is worse off, but B is better off. For example, some people start businesses and sell products at prices below their costs to gain customers. While their customers benefit, the entrepreneur eventually goes out of business. In this situation, others benefit while the entrepreneur doesn't. In organizations we see "sacrificing" situations where individuals engage in innovations that benefit the company (i.e. come up with a way to significantly improve productivity), which might then lead to losing their job (e.g. higher productivity means the need for fewer people and someone needs to go). This is also the situation described at the beginning of the chapter. The owner of the business wants individuals to take risks that would be of value to the organiza-tion, yet the likely outcome of this risk-taking for such individuals is being fired. The upside of the transaction is skewed toward the organization while the employee bears all of the downside.

On the other side of the spectrum is the activity of *theft* (Quadrant T). In this case, A initiates an action where he or she gains but party B loses. Certainly, there are individuals who start businesses that eventually defraud others, where the business doesn't provide benefits to anyone other than the owners. Only the owners win, while everyone else is worse off. We would hope that most of these people go to jail for such actions, but you can probably think of people who personally gained through their actions while others have not. The Madoff, Enron, Tyco, WorldCom, and other corporate scandals are examples of such situations. In addition, individuals engaged in theft can exist in organizations as well. Stock and bond traders might be able to create transactions where these traders generate large bonuses for themselves yet put their organizations in jeopardy. Typically organizations put in significant controls to prevent individuals from creating personal gains that result in everyone else losing.

Finally, we have situations where A initiates an activity that ends up with losses for both A and B. In this case, A *loses* (Quadrant L). People who cause accidents fall into this category. There are also individuals who initiate activities that they hope will be successful but which eventually fail, but fail in a way so that not only does the initiator fail, but so do any others who are involved. Employees, customers, investors, and suppliers are all worse off, too. Again, much like the controls that organizations have on *theft*, organizations tend to monitor employee actions so that organizations are not put in situations that might result in significant harm. Yet, such harm does occur. Recall the story of Jérôme Kerviel, a trader at Société Générale, one of France's largest banks, who managed to evade the bank's controls for nearly a year while he generated 4.9 billion euros in losses for the bank.

Finally, what should be noticed in the framework are the two dotted lines. These lines are points in the framework where wins and/or losses are equal for participants in the transaction. So, in Quadrant E, the dotted line shows where A and B win equally. In Quadrant S, the dotted line shows where A's sacrifices are equal to B's gains.

While this framework may seem to be an oversimplification of interactions between people, it can quickly identify the types of situations that might hinder (or enhance) the incentives (penalties) for individuals to initiate new activities.

IMPLICATIONS FOR ENTREPRENEURIAL RISK-TAKING

As we might imagine, when engaging in activities where we are the recipient of the action outcomes from others, that is, we are the "B" group, either as individuals, organizations, or societies, we want to see individuals in the "A" group engaged in entrepreneuring and sacrificing. In either of these two Quadrants (E and S) the "Bs" are better off. And, conversely, when we are in the "B" group, we seek to minimize transactions where individuals can act engaging in theft or involve us in losing, which make us worse off (Quadrants T and L). When individuals innovate, the "As" in all four quadrants, the goal for them is to seek transactions where they can increase the likelihood that they will be better off (Quadrants T and E), and avoid transactions where they will be worse off (Quadrants S and L).

As we indicated earlier, ideally we would seek to construct situations that result in wins for both parties, "A" and "B." Yet, we find that most organizations want to depend on "sacrificing," actions that put innovators at risk for benefits that they will not likely share in. For example, are most public school teachers really in a position to gain from any benefits that might be generated from innovations in teaching that they might offer? Will innovations in productivity or in student quality result in most public school teachers receiving higher salaries, bonuses, or other incentives? Or will gains in productivity result in fewer teaching jobs? We would surmise that most productivity innovations in education will not result in higher-paid teachers, but rather in fewer teachers (with no higher pay). Given that most teachers are put into a risk/reward structure that mirrors the "sacrificing" quadrant, why would we expect teachers to be innovators? Yet, ironically, most organizations bemoan their lack of "sacrificers" who are willing to take innovative risks.

If the most likely way to increase taking risks to innovate is to design situations where there are wins for the "As" and the "Bs," we suggest that the venture capital model is worth emulating. In the venture capital model, the involvement of individuals in high potential ventures does not mean that these entrepreneurs are risking either a high potential payout, or nothing. Most entrepreneurs are not working for free in their entrepreneurial startups: they receive salaries. In addition, most entrepreneurs involved in high potential ventures are not risking substantial amounts of their own capital. For example, Gartner et al. (in press) found that, on average, founders involved in high potential ventures have approximately $25,000 invested, while founders of low potential ventures have, on average, approximately $5,000 invested in their ventures. In either case, these investments are not substantial: less at risk, financially, than what would be required to purchase a new or used automobile. So, the downside risk for many entrepreneurs involved in high potential ventures would mean that a failure of the venture effort would lead to the loss of the founder's job and the financial amount invested. But those individuals who leave their jobs for another job face some risk that the new position won't work out and that they too could be out of a job.

In the venture capital model, it is the upside of entrepreneurship that warrants the entrepreneur's attention. If a high potential venture succeeds, then the entrepreneur is likely to garner a high salary, and stock in the company that could be worth millions of dollars. Compare choosing the entrepreneur's job to those individuals choosing jobs in organizations. Success at a job as an employee could certainly lead to promotions, higher salaries, bonuses, and the like. But few jobs offer possibilities for earning substantially more through stock and stock options. So, who is taking the risk in their career? When failure in either the "entrepreneurial world" or in the "job world" means pursuing another opportunity (i.e. starting a venture or getting another job—options available to both worlds), then, what is the difference in risk to either group? Given that entrepreneurs may have more potential to earn substantial amounts of money through ownership than workers with jobs, the risk-takers might be individuals who choose to work for someone else. John Morse's perspective could be right.

As noted earlier, entrepreneurial situations vary. The pursuit of some opportunities may have different levels of pay-offs than others, and, the likelihood of these pay-offs may have different probabilities as well. Within that context, there will be different kinds of individuals willing to pursue this entrepreneurial diversity. There is no one profile of entrepreneurial characteristics that determines whether an individual is an entrepreneur, or not. A propensity to take higher levels of risk than others has been shown to not differentiate the entrepreneurs from others. Further, risk-taking propensity doesn't differentiate the successful entrepreneurs from the failures.

Yet, for the most part, entrepreneurs are acting in the expectation of being somewhere in Quadrant E. They expect some personal gain from their actions. We would expect more individuals to engage in innovative actions (which as outsiders we are likely to perceive as "risky") when their actions produce benefits for them. We shouldn't be surprised when few individuals are willing to take risks when they don't see much of a personal upside, and there is a considerable downside.

Entrepreneurship is not about "being" an entrepreneur. Entrepreneurship is about doing what an entrepreneur does: engaging in activities that transform opportunities into viable businesses. It is a matter of perception as to whether entrepreneurial activities are "risky." When one is observing individuals engaged in entrepreneurial activities, it is often a simple matter to fall into the fundamental attribution error: assuming that why entrepreneurs do what they do is determined by who they are.

When involving individuals in entrepreneurial situations that appear to be risky, then, the critical lesson is to evaluate the risks in the situation, rather than worrying about whether the individuals have the necessary propensity to take risks. It is unlikely that many individuals will be willing to undertake entrepreneurial tasks if they perceive these situations as having more negatives than positives. The business owner who plans to fire all of the "failures" will not find many individuals who see the prospect of losing their jobs as a likely outcome of their involvement. When the chance of failure is high, the penalties for failing are significant, and the rewards for success are modest, the likely number of individuals willing to pursue those situations is low. So, while one could look for individuals who prefer low pay-off, high-penalty situations, it might be wiser to change the parameters of the situation. For example, after the recent debacle in the financial markets, it appears that there are an unlimited number of individuals willing to risk other people's money when investment success leads to high pay-off bonuses, and where losing all of an investor's funds leads to no penalty: just a high paying salary. When the rewards for taking risks are high, and the penalties for taking those risks are low, then individuals will engage in risky behaviors. The characteristics of the situation will more likely determine an individual's behaviors than the individual's predisposition for taking risks.

CONCLUSION

So, ask yourself: Does your organization provide rewards commensurate (or greater) than the penalties for engaging in taking risks? Is your organization's reward structure in the *entrepreneuring* quadrant or the *sacrificing*, *theft*, or *losing* quadrants?

This chapter is embedded in a book where other chapters will explore how individuals and organizations utilize various tools to recognize, manage, and change the parameters of "risky" situations. Our mandate was to explore whether entrepreneurs are more prone to engage in risk-taking compared to others. Entrepreneurs are not. Our research has found that entrepreneurs, as a group, are no more prone to risk-taking than the general population, and successful entrepreneurs, as a group, are no more prone to risk-taking than the entrepreneurial "failures." To assume that entrepreneurs take risks because they are "risk-takers" is wrong-headed.

Entrepreneurial risks are undertaken when individuals perceive they can engage in actions that provide rewards that are greater than the perceived likelihood of penalties. While each individual's reward/penalty probabilities and outcomes are different from others, in general the propensity for risk-taking among entrepreneurs is no different than others. So, even though there are entrepreneurs who are, indeed, "risk-takers," there are entrepreneurs who are not. The point is: an individual's predisposition to take risks appears to play a minimal role in most entrepreneurial situations.

REFERENCES

Brockhaus, R. (1980) "Risk Taking Propensity of Entrepreneurs," *Academy of Management Journal*, 23 (3): 509–520.

Cantillon, R. (1755/2001) *Essay on the Nature of Commerce in General*. New Brunswick: Transaction Publishers.

Cipolla, C. M. (1987) "The Basic Laws of Human Stupidity," *Whole Earth Review*, Spring: 2–7.

Gartner, W. B. (1985) "A Framework for Describing and Classifying the Phenomenon of New Venture Creation," *Academy of Management Review*, 10 (4): 696–706.

Gartner, W. B. (1988) "Who is an Entrepreneur? Is the Wrong Question," *American Journal of Small Business*, 12 (4): 11–32.

Gartner, W. B. (2008) "Variations in Entrepreneurship," *Small Business Economics*, 31: 351–361.

Gartner, W. B. and Liao, J. (In press) "Risk Perceptions, Uncertainty and Growth Aspirations as Determinants of Venture Creation Success," *Small Business Economics*.

Gartner, W. B., Frid, C. J., and Alexander, J. C. (In press) "Financing the Emerging Business," *Small Business Economics*.

Gartner, W. B., Shaver, K. G., Carter, N. M., and Reynolds, P. D. (Eds.) (2004) *Handbook of Entrepreneurial Dynamics: The Process of Business Creation*. London: Sage.

Heider, F. (1958) *The Psychology of Interpersonal Relations*. New York: Wiley.

Jackson, D. N. (1976) *Personality Inventory Manual*. Goshen, NY: Research Psychologists Press.

Jones, E. E. and Harris, V. A. (1967) "The Attribution of Attitudes," *Journal of Experimental Social Psychology*, 3: 1–24.

Knight, F. H. (1921) *Risk, Uncertainty and Profit*. Boston: Houghton Mifflin Company.

Kogan, N. and Wallach, M. (1964) *Risk Taking*. New York: Holt, Rinehart and Winston.

Matthew, C. and Human, S. (2004) "The Economic and Community Context for Entrepreneurship: Perceived Environmental Uncertainty," in W. B. Gartner, K. G. Shaver, N. M. Carter, and P. D. Reynolds (Eds.), *Handbook of Entrepreneurial Dynamics*. Thousand Oaks: Sage Publications, 421–429.

Miner, J. B. (1986) *Scoring Guide for the Miner Sentence Completion Scale – Form T*. Eugene: Organizational Measurement Systems Press.

Miner, J. B. and Raju, N. S. (2004) "Risk Propensity Differences between Managers and Entrepreneurs and between Low- and High-Growth Entrepreneurs: A Reply in a more Conservative Vein," *Journal of Applied Psychology*, 89 (1): 3–13.

Morse, J. (1992) Personal Communication.

Reynolds, P. D. and Curtin, R. T. (2004) "Appendix A: Data Collection," in W. B. Gartner, K. G. Shaver, N. M. Carter, and P. D. Reynolds (Eds.), *Handbook of Entrepreneurial Dynamics*. Thousand Oaks: Sage Publications, 453–475.

Ross, L. (1977) "The Intuitive Psychologist and his Shortcomings: Distortions in the Attribution Process," in L. Berkowitz (Ed.), *Advances in Experimental Social Psychology*, Vol. 10. New York: Academic Press, 173–220.

Say, J. (1880/1971) *A Treatise on Political Economy: Or the Production, Distribution and Consumption of Wealth.* Translated by C. R. Prinsep and Clement C. Biddle. New York: Augustus M. Kelley.

Stewart, W. H. and Roth, P. L. (2001) "Risk Propensity Differences between Entrepreneurs and Managers: A Meta-analytic Review," *Journal of Applied Psychology*, 86 (1): 145–153.

Stewart, W. H. and Roth, P. L. (2004) "Data Quality Affects Meta-analytic Conclusions: A Response to Miner and Raju (2004) Concerning Entrepreneurial Risk Propensity," *Journal of Applied Psychology*, 89 (1): 14–21.

Steyaert, C. (2007) "'Entrepreneuring' as a Conceptual Attractor? A Review of Process Theories in 20 Years of Entrepreneurship Studies," *Entrepreneurship and Regional Development*, 19 (6): 453–477.

Wallach, M. and Kogan, N. (1959) "Sex Differences and Judgment Processes," *Journal of Personality*, 27: 555–564.

Wallach, M. and Kogan, N. (1961) "Aspects of Judgment and Decision-making: Interrelationships and Changes with Age," *Behavioral Science*, 6: 23–36.

Xu, H. and Ruef, M. (2004) "The Myth of the Risk-tolerant Entrepreneur," *Strategic Organization*, 2 (4): 331–355.

PART II

Managing Unruly Reality: Risks from the Business Environment

When a management with a reputation for brilliance tackles a business with a reputation for bad economics, it is the reputation of the business that remains intact.

Warren Buffett

INFANTRY PLATOON LEADERS and fighter pilots know that a rapid and effective decision cycle holds the key to survival. This street wisdom, which has become known as the observe-orient-decide-act cycle (or, more commonly, as the OODA Loop) can also offer a framework for survival in the competitive marketplace. Its essential activities are:

- Observation: discerning new information and selecting from a sea of factoids those most relevant to the success of the venture.
- Orientation: placing these observations in the context of the competitive environment and the internal strengths and weaknesses of the venture.
- Decision: choosing a course of action, always provisional depending on the results.
- Action: implementing that decision and observing the outcomes—then recycling the process based on the new understanding.

The logic of combat rewards a decision cycle that is more rapid than the opponents' and that yields better judgments. The logic of innovation and entrepreneurship rewards the same, but with an important distinction: the business environment in place when the new venture is conceived can change markedly as the business grows, and once-comfortable assumptions can set traps for the unwary. To illustrate, consider the case of Motorola's entrepreneurial venture, *Iridium*, which began with bright promise in the late 1980s and ended in financial ruin a decade later.

IRIDIUM AND THE HAZARDS OF THE BUSINESS ENVIRONMENT: A CAUTIONARY TALE

The vision was compelling and for 1987 extraordinarily bold: instant and affordable voice communication on a single network from any place on the globe to any other place. And it came just as Motorola began to understand correctly the implications of the end of the Cold War for its defense satellite business. The vision would be implemented by using the satellite communication capabilities developed for national security to build a commercial network so powerful that a customer on safari could call his stockbroker from the jungles of Africa or the crest of the Himalayas.

And so Motorola set out on a 10-year technology and infrastructure campaign to realize the vision. The project would be managed through a spin-off company, *Iridium*, named after the 77th element in the Periodic Table because the founders thought that 77 satellites would be required for the mature network. By late 1997, enough satellites were in orbit to begin limited service, and Vice President Al Gore placed the first phone call from the White House to the great grandson of Alexander Graham Bell in Virginia. By the time that commercial service was announced a year later, about $2 billion had been invested in the project.

The technology and political challenges that *Iridium* overcame to put this all in place had been formidable—but that triumph had come at a price. An intensely focused *Iridium* had paid little attention to events outside the company, and the world had not bothered to await the *Iridium* network. Improvements in microelectronics enabled the transition from "car phones" to "mobile phones," and expanded the range of services that these could provide. At the same time, the ground-based cellular network could grow in modular fashion, tower by tower. Unlike *Iridium*, competitors could offer services before their entire cellular network was in place, thus securing early customers and revenue. The modular expansion also kept capital expenditures at a manageable pace.

As a consequence, *Iridium* was simply not competitive for most customers— overpriced and with inferior service in urban areas—by the time it announced full commercial service in November of 1998. By August of 1999 *Iridium* lacked sufficient customers and had little prospect for more; the company sought financial restructuring through Chapter 11, and ended commercial service in March of 2000. The deeply discounted assets were purchased by private investors who have since made a profitable business serving the segment of the communications market that truly needs communication from mountaintop to jungle—mining and petroleum operations, search and rescue, and ironically, national defense. But neither did the new owners have to purchase the infrastructure at full price.

We offer this small "morality tale" to illustrate the hazards that arise from failure to learn from the business environment and adapt. We now explore that environment in greater depth.

THE BUSINESS ENVIRONMENT

We can think of any venture as surrounded by two kinds of external environment, both of which influence its success, albeit in different ways. The first is a "Transaction Environment," illustrated in Figure II.1, in which persons and institutions hold direct transactional relationships with the enterprise.

In the case of employees, for example, the transactions might be formal agreements; in the case of regulators, legal requirements; and in the case of customers, informal but equally powerful expectations. But the most powerful and immediate influence is exercised by the investors, who govern the new venture directly through Boards of Directors and covenants built into the investment term sheets. The management team can influence the quality and effectiveness of these relationships, but never fully control them. Controlled or not, the success of the venture remains tightly coupled to them.

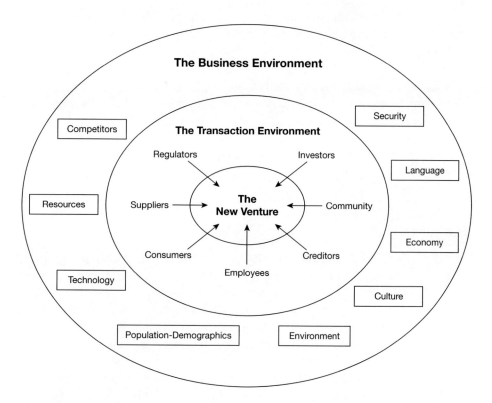

Figure II.1. The Business Environment

Beyond the *transactions environment* lies the *business environment,* a domain of influence less malleable to management, but equally powerful in shaping the success of the new venture. Consider the workforce, for example. Labor laws and contractual arrangements, which dwell within the realm of transactions, are immediate and visible. Yet environmental influences beyond the reach of management ultimately set the pace of workforce achievement: the state of the economy (high or low unemployment, interest rates, and so forth), the cultural norms (whether achievement is valued, work ethic, and the like), and educational levels (functional illiteracy and innumeracy). All these influence the ability of the workforce to build a positive *business environment* for the new venture.

During times when the *business environment* remains stable—as in the electric utility industry of the 1950s and 1960s, for example—standard forecasting methods provide a reasonable basis for planning and budgeting. But during periods of instability—the electric utility industry of the 1970s, for example—standard planning tools and the institutional knowledge that supports them can become a trap. Consider the growing influence of technology, which spills outside the boundaries of our established business models—who would have thought of Nokia as the world's largest camera company? In a dynamic, technology-driven business environment, the strengths that served companies so well in a more stable world become liabilities:

- A hierarchical culture competes poorly with the more open culture because command authority can discourage the ongoing heresies needed for creativity and innovation.
- Lengthy technology development campaigns add to overhead costs and risk developing projects for a market that has long since passed.
- And institutional skill sets that serve well when customer needs can be predicted, can become blind to the emerging realities of the technology marketplace.

Thus, innovation managers and entrepreneurs need a systematic way to understand decision-making in an unruly business environment.

DECISION-MAKING IN A DYNAMIC BUSINESS ENVIRONMENT

The customary vocabulary of risk does not help us to understand or manage it because the language blurs important distinctions about what can be inferred from experience and what cannot. Consider Figure II.2, which summarizes the full domain of what is conversationally termed "risk" by organizing it according to: (a) our ability to recognize events that pose a threat to the enterprise and estimate the likelihood that they will occur; and (b) our ability to understand the outcomes of such events should they occur (Awerbuch et al. 2006).

The northwest quadrant of Figure II.2 holds the domain of what can properly be called *risk*. For the kinds of decision-making that apply here, analysts can find a reasonable basis for estimating the likelihood of a hazardous event and for

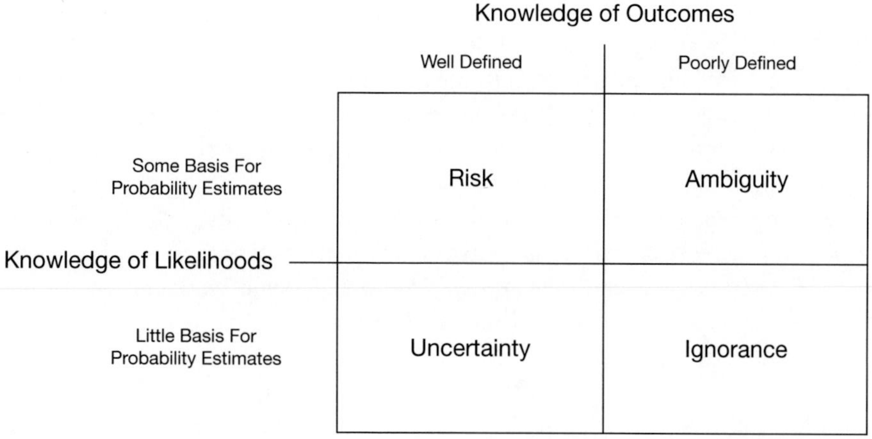

Knowledge of Outcomes

	Well Defined	Poorly Defined
Some Basis For Probability Estimates	Risk	Ambiguity
Little Basis For Probability Estimates	Uncertainty	Ignorance

Knowledge of Likelihoods

Figure II.2. The Domains of Likelihood and Outcomes

understanding its consequences should it occur. Historical experience serves well as the basis for probability estimates, and provides a reasonable guide to the future. Here the business environment behaves predictably, or can be reasonably presumed to do so, which enables sophisticated analyses from the probability data. Consider, for example, how the U.S. Congressional Budget Office uses Monte Carlo analysis to project alternative financial futures for Social Security. The demographic properties are statistically stable; and the chief source of volatility, Congressional actions to change the system, is dispatched by assuming that either the current policies or an assumed alternative hold into an indefinite future. This is the domain of the probability distribution, and properly so. But we should not entertain the illusion that it applies equally well to the entrepreneurial venture—it does not.

For those launching a new enterprise, the most important decisions do not reside within the narrow domain of risk. Indeed, events beyond the range of historical experience and unknowable at the time that a decision must be made often emerge to influence its outcome. These possibilities cannot properly be labeled "risk" because neither their probabilities nor their outcomes can be understood in advance. They occupy the domain of *ignorance*, the southeast quadrant of Figure II.2. Consider, for example, political uprisings such as those in Tunisia, Egypt, and Libya during the spring of 2011. A small army of highly paid consultants and intelligence analysts failed to predict these, and the likelihood of a stable outcome remains unknowable. Such political volatility sharply influences the price of oil, and hence the prospects for new ventures whose success rises or falls with the price of oil.

The other domains in Figure II.2 simply add to the black hole of *ignorance*: (a) an understanding of likelihood (but not the outcomes)—the domain of *ambiguity*; or (b) an understanding of outcomes (but not likelihood)—the domain of *uncertainty*.

COPING WITH UNRULY REALITY

How then should entrepreneurs and innovators manage risk in an unruly business environment? Plainly, the passage of time eventually reveals the essential character of any hazard. Whether the hurricane will strike tomorrow and with what consequence can be forecast today, though not precisely. By the end of the week, however, all that will be known—only to be replaced by other unknowns about the future. Similarly, the passage of enough time will illuminate each present-day hazard, and eventually reveal what should have been done if perfect foresight had been granted the decision-maker. But to say "eventually" is to say "irrelevant": the essential problem is that appropriate actions must be taken before the innovator or entrepreneur can know that they are really appropriate.

In Part II, three chapters address ways to cope with the unruly realities of innovation and entrepreneurship. In Chapter 3, "Learning from the Unexpected," Dr. Rita Gunther McGrath of Columbia University shows how entrepreneurs and innovators can use unanticipated events, those that prove fortunate and (especially) those less so, to learn better ways to achieve success. To be sure, this learning often conflicts with the imperatives of the planning and budgeting cycle. Still, plans must be made and budgets set. And so, the real challenge is to balance the need for learning with the need for plan-based management and accountability. Unlike the old camp motto, "Clean mind, clean body—take your pick," the successful innovator really must achieve both.

In Chapter 4, "Evidence-Based Management for Entrepreneurial Environments," Dr. Jeffrey Pfeffer of Stanford University views the persistently high failure rates for new ventures through a different lens: the failure to use effectively the available evidence. He makes the case that evidence-based decision-making could improve the success rates experienced by new ventures and by their investors. And finally, in Chapter 5, "Betting the Farm," Dr. David L. Bodde shows how real options analysis and scenario planning can help entrepreneurs and corporate innovators manage the big bets that often accompany new technology ventures.

We respectfully commend their thinking to you as you consider the risks that come unbidden from the business environment.

REFERENCES

Awerbuch, S., Stirling, A. C., Jansen J., and Beurskens, L. (2006) "Portfolio and Diversity Analysis of Energy Technologies Using Full-Spectrum Risk Measures," in D. Bodde, K. Leggio, and M. Taylor (Eds.), *Managing Enterprise Risk: What the Electric Industry Experience Implies for Contemporary Business.* Elsevier Topics in Global Energy Economics, Regulation and Policy, pp. 202–222.

Chapter 3

Learning from the Unexpected

RITA GUNTHER MCGRATH

INTRODUCTION: UNEXPECTED EVENTS AND THE TENSION BETWEEN PLANNING AND LEARNING

WHY IS IT THAT MOST established organizations create beautifully institutionalized systems that guarantee their members will suffer from *systemic learning disabilities*? Why are the indicators that investors use to judge whether a new venture is on track often *inimical* to the very learning needed to find a successful path forward? The culprit, ironically, is often the commitment to the milestones, results, and incentives in an agreed-upon plan that was laid out in advance. The resulting tension between planning and learning is one that bedevils the many entrepreneurs and executives who are seeking to capitalize on new opportunities in highly uncertain environments.

Planning to Learn versus Planning to be "Right"

The fundamental dilemma is that industrial-age notions of what constitutes good management and effective entrepreneurship slip without conscious recognition into the evaluation of what constitutes a positive outcome. For instance, for decades, textbooks have encouraged managers to "manage by exception" in which deviations from expected results are characterized as negative. Likewise, entrepreneurs are widely encouraged to prepare business plans to acquire the support or endorsement of financial backers and other stakeholders. In all these cases, a good outcome is when results match previous expectations. Good managers are "right." Or, as was relayed to me in the context of a discussion of barriers to innovation in a large corporation, "you need to understand that around here, we don't plan to learn—we plan to win!"

Missing the Signals

In many organizations, deviating from plan is seen as highly negative, even if the deviation is in a positive direction. This can cause even promising opportunities to be overlooked. Success, too, can lead us to ignore interesting new information because we aren't in the market for it. And all people have cognitive biases that tend to keep valuable new information away from us. At the same time, whether for an established organization or for a new enterprise, its ability to learn from new, unexpected information is a highly valuable strategic asset, one that is worth spending time to develop.

By definition, growth requires that organizations venture to some extent into unexpected territory, whether that is a corporation seeking innovations or new companies seeking to open new territory. Thus, for entrepreneurs and leaders of growth, helping organizations learn from the unexpected requires an adroit balance of the demands of reliable performance and planning—and the opportunities represented by unexpected events. While the need to promote and foster discovery has long been emphasized, particularly in entrepreneurial contexts, embracing the concept has proven challenging.[1]

BARRIERS TO BENEFITTING FROM UNEXPECTED EVENTS

Learning and Implicit Contracts

The concept of the learning organization became very popular in the 1990s, as advocates stressed that a key leadership skill was the ability to *facilitate learning.*[2] For all the good press, however, being a learning organization is difficult to master in practice. Part of the problem is that learning contradicts many organizational practices. Learning is a process that involves testing assumptions and seeking to discover their limits. Most work in organizations involves operating on the basis of assumptions, but seeking to confirm their correctness. Even for entrepreneurs, the need to convincingly and passionately advocate for their own business plans can prevent them from seeing any of the potential ways the future might not be consistent with their predictions.

A significant challenge to learning from the unexpected has to do with the way implicit contracts are created through corporate budgeting processes and the allocation of funds to entrepreneurial ventures. In a typical scenario, a team that wants to do something new prepares a sales pitch to some funding authority. The presentation is carefully orchestrated, with beautifully crafted PowerPoint slides and oodles of spreadsheets, projecting what the new business will do in its first five years of successful existence. Assumptions on which the plan is based are often listed. If the pitch is compelling enough, the venture raises funding. That's where the trouble starts. Executives in the company are implicitly investing in a project plan whose promise is to execute against the activities specified before the project was even started.

The difficulties begin when the plan encounters reality. Inevitably, things turn out to be different than what was anticipated. In an effective learning process, these deviations would be welcomed as valuable inputs to determining the course of action that will eventually succeed, even if it means parting from the plan. All too often, however, the unexpected comes to be seen as the enemy. Rather than adapting the plan to unfolding reality, venture teams strive to make that plan come true, because that is what they committed to do in the budgeting process. The result is that vast resources can be spent trying to enforce the reality of a plan that had considerable uncertainty in it from the start. Of course, eventually reality will always win, with the frequent outcome that the entire venture is regarded as a flop. Once it attains that status, nobody wants to revisit the decisions and learning that took place, resulting in a dead loss.

Routine Processes in Organizations are Unconsciously Maintained

It is quite common in organizations that the mental models upon which plans are based are not explicit. Instead, what was once a theory—an exciting discovery, or a deep insight—becomes forgotten, while the actions taken based on it become embedded in practices and procedures.[3] The practices and procedures might endure, but their original source, the underlying theory, is no longer explicitly remembered. Worse, the practices often replicate beyond their point of origin and are utilized under conditions that in some cases make little sense. When reality diverges from plan in such situations, it may not even be noticed because actions based on the plan are no longer referencing the original reason it was adopted.

At DuPont, for instance, a powerful culture of safety evolved from the company's origins as a manufacturer of explosives. As associated practices became embedded in this culture, they evolved, becoming part of the taken for granted way that all work was done. DuPonters, for instance, are instructed to hold the handrail while walking up or down stairs (which can be quite amusing if a group of people are heading upstairs or down at the same time). A meeting at DuPont would never proceed with the tangle of cords and equipment plugs littering the floor of a typical meeting room— no way. Loose cords are taped down, possible uneven surfaces marked, and everyone is encouraged to be mindful. Meetings always begin with a safety topic, including the location of exit doors and any procedures to be used in case of emergency. If you worked for DuPont you wouldn't think any of this was unusual. Indeed, you would take for granted that safety consciousness would be part of any plan you developed.

It would not be until someone from DuPont had the opportunity to contrast their safety oriented behavior with the practices that go on in other companies that it would become clear that their culture of safety is indeed exceptional. The exceptional nature of the safety culture, revealed by the unexpected behavior of other organizations, might well provoke a "learning" response. Indeed, one of the dilemmas of the safety culture is that it is so embedded that those seeking to encourage the organization to take more risks find that the safety culture dominates even the calculated risk-taking needed for learning in new environments.

The Rigidity of Conventional Corporate Planning

In a traditional corporate planning structure, good managers meet their plans, make their numbers, and are right about what the future holds. Unlike a scientist, who is trained to look for anomalies and departures from preconceived theory, in corporations we seek to reinforce the correctness of our plan. If you think about it, isn't this a recipe guaranteed to prevent individuals from recognizing unexpected opportunities? It presumes that there is no need to embed learning into the planning process.

This observation led to the core idea behind "discovery driven" planning in which the goal is not to prove that one was right; but rather to make carefully considered investments in learning to find out what the correct answer is.[4] Conventional planning has a lot to answer for. In the course of my research, I've studied literally hundreds of major corporate and entrepreneurial flops, and in each case, the plans underlying the ventures failed to include substantial amounts of testing.

The pattern for such corporate debacles is similar. Consider, for example, the ill-fated effort by Motorola in the 1990s to offer a truly global mobile phone. At the time the venture was conceived, in the mid-1980s, mobile phones were in their infancy. One may recall the 1988 movie *Wall Street* in which to show how much money had been procured by his nefarious ways, the villainous Gordon Gecko was pictured talking on a huge mobile phone. The image, of a large phone that was expensive to use, reflected the limits of the technology and networks of the time. At that time, also, there were no standards for mobile communication, such advances as cross-network roaming were still years away, and the only real users of mobile phones were those who really needed them because the technology was so expensive. Motorola conceived of a brilliant plan that would overcome the obstacles to worldwide coverage—to surround the earth with a network of low-earth-orbit satellites that would "walk" calls from one to the other. The plan to create this venture—dubbed the *Iridium* project— was approved in 1990. Throughout the 1990s, Motorola and the *Iridium* consortium it led spent time raising money and launching satellites. The marketing and market size assumptions in their plans, however, didn't change. This, despite the reality that GSM became the global standard in Europe and many other countries in the early 1990s, roaming made much of the differentiation of the *Iridium* offer irrelevant, and that satellite technology was not really the best choice for business-people once other alternatives existed because the phones didn't work in moving automobiles, inside office buildings, or in many large cities!

The team behind the *Iridium* project never even tried to confirm or disconfirm the assumptions in the plan. Instead, the project was managed as though they were working with facts, when in fact there was an enormous amount of learning to be done throughout the decade they spent working on the program. Much of this learning could have been done through trials, experiments, and mockups, yet the planning structures in place did not encourage such behavior.

This is a common pattern in many such conventionally planned projects. Typically, in a large organization the proponents of a new venture assemble a proposal that includes a business plan and description of how it will generate enormous ROI if the corporation only funds the plan. Funds received, the venture leaders head off to implement their ideas, only to discover that reality and their plans do not necessarily correspond. The problem then is that they feel compelled to try to make the plan come true, treating it as a commitment to act, rather than a set of hypotheses to test.

Entrepreneurs can fall into similar traps, although they don't tend to be able to lose quite so much money as an established organization as a general rule. Instead of seeking to find information that their business idea might not come to fruition, many will persist in trying to develop it long past the point at which evidence has built up that it might be better to move on. This can be exacerbated if they have spent the money of the early backers, the "friends family and fools" that provide the early resources for many an entrepreneurial venture.

ENABLING LEARNING PRACTICES

Fortunately, it is possible to overcome some of these challenges and pursue practices that are associated with beneficial learning from unexpected events. They do not require a total cultural makeover or drastic restructuring, and can often be implemented fairly easily. They do, however, require a different mindset and a different set of disciplines about acting strategically under conditions of significant uncertainty. It is somewhat paradoxical—one wants to be optimistic and positive about the prospects of a fledgling business, while at the same time remaining open to unexpected, disconfirming evidence that a different course of action might be more fruitful.

Contrast the desire for predictable outcomes with the approach people would take if they were seeking to build up a body of scientific knowledge. Scientists draw on the work of those who came before them to develop a theory, which is simply a set of beliefs about what causes what and why. Scientific research, which can span a range of activities from simple observation to experimentation, seeks to enrich and extend the theory. Hypotheses that are not supported can still be useful, particularly if they are surprising, as they suggest alternative explanations and routes for new research.[5]

For new ventures and entrepreneurs, in contrast, resources are given to those working on projects about which they are hopeful. The goal is not to find out where your idea doesn't work, but rather to prove to the world that it does. It isn't so much that the data are not there, rather that in a context of advocacy, that they are not sought out. Often, people perceive that they will not be rewarded unless their project goes forward; indeed, that they will suffer in terms of career or reputation if it doesn't.

Effective learning, in contrast, might reflect a process closer to that of scientific theory building. A first key notion is that the theory of the case—the "what will cause what to happen"—needs to be clear and explicit. The second is that testing the theory calls for specific observational or experimental processes that can lead the learner to conclude that their suppositions (hypotheses, if you will) are either supported or not. In other words, learners seek to find out whether the logic of causality that they have supposed to be true fits with some empirical pattern or outcome. Finally, the theory is updated to reflect increased understanding, or new theories are developed in the face of conflicting or unexpected results.

Thus, Pfizer's researchers discovered that a drug they had hypothesized might help heart disease victims didn't work, but that it did create unexpected and most interesting side effects, leading to their blockbuster erectile dysfunction drug, Viagra. Had they not been looking to test clearly stated hypotheses about the drug's effects and been surprised, the unexpectedly favorable discovery may never have been made.

Plan to the Limits of Your Knowledge; then Replan

Learning from the unexpected calls for a shift in mindset from one in which making plans and being right is the goal to one in which converting assumptions to knowledge is the goal. The tone for this is set by the way the progress is measured, by metrics and reward mechanisms, and by the way the founding team or senior managers focus their attention. When moving into uncharted territory, the notion of differentiating between assumptions and knowledge is key. Progress can thus be measured by the amount of evidence gathered that supports certain critical assumptions and by the extent to which an organization is able to make better decisions, rather than by marketplace success. Such a mindset paves the way for the acceptance of surprising discoveries.

One practice, well known to experienced entrepreneurs, is to establish checkpoints when one has reached the limit of what one can confidently plan for and review the major assumptions in the plan. Consider the early days of the Internet: a number of assumptions about how the Internet would work came to be taken for granted, despite the fact that they were completely unproven. Some of these assumptions—that information had to be free, that eyeballs could easily be monetized, and that effective barriers to the digitization of electronic content could be erected—have proven to be highly damaging to industries as varied as news organizations, music companies, and even Internet service providers (AOL comes to mind).[6]

Unexpectedly, Apple turned out to be able to violate both the assumption that content would be free and that it could not be protected, creating a formidable new business model by flying in the face of what was conventional wisdom with its iTunes and iPod music-playing combination. This franchise was extended to incorporate now-popular "apps" with Apple's iPhone device. Only now are news organizations such as the *New York Times* coming to grips with the unexpected result that their revenues from their digital platforms would never compensate for the lost advertising revenue of their printed versions. Indeed, as of this writing the *Times* has announced that it is rejecting the "news should be free" model in favor of returning to charging for its content.

Today, as the Internet evolves, observers are now considering the implications of a number of unexpected developments. For instance, rather than the assumption that web pages are the fundamental units of information to be accessed via search, tagging individual fields may radically change the nature of search. Rather than the assumption that everyone shares a similar way to access the web, instead we are confronting the implications of a splintering of the user experience as people use devices other than computers for access. Further, as individuals' interactions on the web increasingly have a social networking dimension, the economics of such areas as search and advertising may shift dramatically. And as advertisers develop new technologies capable of piercing anonymity on the web, unknown social and behavioral reactions are likely. Google's Eric Schmidt has recently said (in jest, one hopes) that people will abandon their previous identities at the age of 18 to escape the consequences of youthful indiscretions.

Planning to Incorporate "Intelligent" Failures and Disconfirming Evidence

Surprisingly, a considerable body of research has concluded that failure in some form is absolutely essential to organizational learning. My colleague Sim Sitkin, for example, argues that failure creates a recognition of risk and a motivation for change that would otherwise not exist. Without failures, organizations simply do not have the raw material that they need to motivate the search for better solutions. Not all failures, however, are equally useful to provoke learning from the unexpected. Instead, Sitkin developed a concept he termed "intelligent failures," which have the following five characteristics:

> (1) They result from thoughtfully *planned actions* that (2) have *uncertain outcomes*, (3) are *modest* in scale, (4) are executed and responded to with *alacrity* (eagerness), and (5) take place in domains that are *familiar* enough to permit effective learning.[7]

To return to the analogy of the knowledge-creating scientist, learning from intelligent failures is a powerful way for entrepreneurial people to develop ever-better theories and ever-better practices. Such learning, however, cannot take place in an environment in which small failures are covered up or go unnoticed. Instead, the objective is to bring such modest mishaps to the attention of people in a position to do something about them, often preventing major failures that can occur subsequently.

Sometimes, organizations actually design structures so that the consequences of operational or execution failures never reach the attention of those in a position to make systemic corrections. Consider the organization with a fantastic complaint department. While customers may be mollified at their excellent treatment, the problems that generated complaints go unnoticed in the parts of the organization where the root problem could be solved. And, of course, decision-makers are often remote from the operational activities that could allow them to learn from intelligent failures.

A powerful way to provoke positive learning is to design small-scale organizational experiments with the goal of testing carefully articulated business processes. Companies design experiments all the time, of course, in the form of pilots, beta-tests or prototypes. Yet often the so-called "experiments" are either created in such a way that they support a preconceived notion or they do not genuinely test a clearly articu-lated set of hypotheses about a given situation.

Design firm IDEO, in contrast, is extremely deliberate about the insight it seeks to obtain from the experiments it runs for its clients. The prototyping processes they have created are deliberately designed to yield unexpected outcomes with the goal of fostering learning and understanding of boundary conditions. The firm is a proponent of extensive prototyping (both of products and of experiences) in order to get better and better feedback from potentially important players. The prototypes are constructed in such a way that they can be "broken" (as one of their principals told me), thus illuminating the point at which a particular theory stops working. This is a great illustration of the process of generating intelligent failures at low cost.

Small-scale failures can also help overcome the confirmation bias.[8] The confirmation bias reflects decision-makers' natural tendency to absorb and rely on information that supports their previously held assumptions—that confirms them—and reject new data that are not consistent with their previously held beliefs. Unfortunately, the confirmation bias can prevent your even noticing disconfirming evidence. A simple question that is effective in combating the bias is to ask at key checkpoints, "What new information would cause us to change our minds about this issue?" and to give people permission to identify such information (if it exists). Simply recognizing the risk of falling into the confirmation bias can create a far more learning-friendly mindset in your organization.

Intelligent Planning and Budgeting

Rather than budget all at once for a project and then assume it is based on facts, a more sensible approach is to link the investment of resources to the learning challenges of the venture. Small amounts of funding might be budgeted for learning investments, such as marketing studies, prototypes, or customer experience investigations. If, and only if, these prove fruitful, are funds released for more substantive investments. The goal is sequenced release of resources rather than all-at-once budgeting. Indeed, venture capitalists use this approach when they allocate funds to ventures as they achieve increasingly ambitious milestones.

The theory behind this point of view about budgeting I've called "real options reasoning."[9] It reflects the idea that firms can create valuable opportunities by making small investments today that convey the right, but not the obligation, to make further investments. The advantage of this approach is that the risk to the organization is known at any point in time, yielding the opportunity for the organization to engage in low-cost experimentation while it determines the most promising route to realizing benefits from the project.

Using External Learning Arenas to Enrich Venture Plans

Another change to conventional planning practices is to encourage those designing plans to learn from the experiences of others. A type of learning that you might think of as learning from co-opted experiences extends the reach of the organization to benefit from lessons learned by others. Procter & Gamble has famously engaged in this practice with an approach it calls "connect and develop." The concept is that leaders at P&G need to look aggressively outside the boundaries of the organization for new practices and ideas that it might in turn commercialize. An early example of this approach was its acquisition of "Dr. John's Spinbrush," a product that was subsequently relabeled the "Crest" Spinbrush and which successfully created a whole category of budget-priced electrically powered toothbrushes. It is worth noting that an enormous amount of political and bridge-building work needed to be done by the leaders involved for the acquisition to find an accepting home within the monolithic P&G brand structure.

A more targeted mechanism for learning from the unexpected is through access to problem-solving networks. One of the more interesting approaches is deployed by open innovation companies such as InnoCentive. On the InnoCentive website, organizations with problems to be solved ("seekers") advertise their issue and what they would pay for someone to come up with the answer. Individuals and companies that believe they may have a way of addressing the problem ("solvers") submit their proposed solutions. If the solution is accepted, the seeker gets a thorny problem resolved and the solver receives the monetary reward. An interesting aspect of the InnoCentive network is that often solutions are found from unexpected places. Thus, a challenge that a firm might normally address with skills drawn from chemistry might be solved by someone developing a biological solution. An advantage of marketplaces like this is that such serendipitous discoveries can be facilitated.

Exchanges such as InnoCentive and other "open" marketplaces that link people and ideas or that support so-called "crowdsourcing" have flourished as organizations seek to benefit by gaining insights beyond their boundaries.

A great deal of organizational learning also takes place as people that work in firms observe what other firms are doing, and as people move from firm to firm, thus facilitating learning from the experiences of others. Learning from others' mistakes (or successes) can be a cost-effective way of creating better outcomes. Here, however, it is important to distinguish again between gaining real knowledge and simply adopting the same widespread assumptions that multiple organizations have. Many executives have come to regret decisions made based on the fact that other firms had adopted a particular practice, without necessarily having a basis of fact to go on. In the disastrous bidding for 3G network spectrum, for instance, many executives justified their decisions because other players in the industry were bidding.

Alternatively, firms can benefit by examining the failures of others. For example, despite many leading firms encouraging the development of tablet-style devices that would free users from the traditional keyboard and mouse of the personal computer era, the technologies never achieved widespread adoption. All those earlier disappointments, however, eventually suggested to firms such as Apple what a touch-screen enabled device would have to do to achieve mass market potential, enabling the company to benefit from the earlier, failed attempts of others.

Another, and sometimes overlooked, arena for learning is what you might think of as learning from thought experiments. Techniques such as simulations and model-building are examples of tools that can facilitate figuring out where a system might behave in an unexpected way, allowing for better decision-making. Detecting how a hurricane might affect property values and how insurance for homes in hurricane-vulnerable areas should be priced is a problem that requires model-building, with the assumptions in the model made explicit. The model can simulate a variety of different conditions. To the extent that some of the outcomes are surprising, a firm such as Swiss Reinsurance can refine its pricing and coverages over time. Indeed, many systems that are too complex to model in real life can benefit from simulated modeling.

LEADERSHIP PRACTICES

The actions of its leaders have an enormous impact on an organization's propensity to take in new information from unexpected sources and utilize this information effectively. Leaders and entrepreneurs who are themselves curious, who ask questions, and who encourage their people to identify alternatives and to go beyond standard sources are making it clear that they value learning. On the other hand, leaders who are impatient for a quantifiable answer, for "proof" and for "facts," signal that new information may not be all that valuable to them.

Listen when You'd Least Like to

One of the deadliest signals a leader can send from a learning perspective is that new information that might presage a threat to the existing business is not welcome. A vivid example is offered of Eldridge Reeves Johnson, a brilliant inventor and entrepreneur who founded the Victor Talking Machine Company of Camden, New Jersey. In its day, the Victor organization essentially owned its markets—it was hugely successful with the upper middle class who enjoyed what for the time was high fidelity sound in their own living rooms. But new developments were afoot, particularly a new way of transmitting sounds, radio. Johnson was not having any part of this potentially disruptive influence on his business. As an observer later recounted:

> Imagine *radio* as a dirty word. Once, when radio was a hot new medium as exciting and unpredictable as the Internet is today, it was cursed by the very company that should have most embraced it—the Victor Talking Machine Co., of Camden, NJ. Victor was then one of the greatest entrepreneurial success stories of the day, but its owner didn't understand how the world was changing. So, ironically, in 1924, the company shunned one of the richest opportunities of its age. Just as the home radio set was fueling the greatest consumer technology revolution in decades, a new employee at Victor was warned not to even utter the word *radio* while on the premises.[10]

Clearly, Johnson was not going to encourage very much learning about this brave new world. It eventually proved his undoing, as Victor was snapped up by the Radio Corporation of America, whose CEO, David Sarnoff, was mostly interested in the company's manufacturing and distribution capabilities. The lesson is that often the unexpected information that a leader least wishes to embrace is crucial to the organization's survival.

Be Decisive about Redirecting Launches

As with any capability-building effort, building the capacity to learn from the unexpected in your organization benefits from clarity with respect to what kind of learning is welcome in which contexts. One particular distinction has to do with the extent to which an endeavor is highly uncertain. As I've argued, projects that expose the organization to high levels of uncertainty are best managed as "real options." Options are very useful and have an important role to play in the course of an organization's strategy. The dilemma is that nobody makes money from options that go unexercised. At some point, a decision must be made to go forward and engage in the launch of an initiative.

Once the launch decision is made, the organization is effectively investing to exercise the option. While learning is still enormously important, because the risks tend to increase as an offering, careful monitoring of whether the project is on track and whether it needs to be redirected is hugely important. If the launch doesn't go as planned, the leader needs to be prepared to decisively change course, particularly if outcomes depart in a meaningful way from previous expectations.

Two examples of organizations that had to change course after launching significant strategic initiatives are Sweden's IKEA and U.S.-based Amazon.com. In IKEA's case, despite a several-decades-long record of success selling flat-packed, beautifully designed furniture to budget-conscious young people, the launch of their IKEA Concept in the United States was less than auspicious. As one case about the company reported:

> the company discovered that Americans did not like its products: apparently, its beds and kitchen cabinets did not fit American sheets and appliances, its sofas were too hard for American comfort, its product dimensions were in centimeters rather than inches, and its kitchenware was too small for American serving-size preferences. As one manager recalled, "People told us they were drinking out of the vases."[11]

Faced with unambiguous evidence of lack of customer acceptance (another manager quipped "I can't understand why Americans won't redesign their windows to fit our curtains"), IKEA's leaders initiated a major redesign of its offerings intended for the American market, a huge shift for a company that had previously endeavored to keep as much global similarity as possible.

Amazon.com similarly went through several difficult learning experiences with its move into third party selling (in which the company sells goods produced by other companies and takes a commission on the sale). Its initial foray into third party selling was to offer auction services in 1999. Designed to compete with web giant eBay, the offering was never well received by customers. Later that year, it tried to sell fixed-price goods from third parties in a separate section of the website, called "Z-shops." This didn't work. In 2001, the company began to feature products from third parties with a used book exchange. That was well received. Eventually, Amazon began to feature third party goods right on their main search pages, an experiment that horrified some of its own buyers. But as CEO Jeff Bezos argues,

> My observation on that would be that it's important to be stubborn on the vision and flexible on the details. I talked about the evolution of our market-place business—that's a good example of where we were relentless on the vision. We made a lot of twists and turns in the execution. We worked on it for a few years. But we didn't give up on the vision.[12]

Similar investments in learning have been made to launch Amazon into other adjacent businesses, such as "Amazon Web Services," which allows customers to use Amazon's computing capacity to quickly scale up (or down) their own computing needs. These offers are a great example of how a company found new revenue growth by commercializing activities that it needed to master for its own operations.

Consider Both Sins of Omission and of Commission

In many organizations, employees learn through often painful experience that trying and failing is far more apt to earn them a punishment than not trying at all. This refers to a common tendency to punish sins of commission (trying and failing) while ignoring sins of omission (failing to try at all). Punishing experiments while neglecting inaction is a recipe guaranteed to squelch learning. For one thing, implicitly encouraging people not to try new things for fear of something going wrong limits the natural experimental process, which might lead to valuable new discoveries. For another, it tends to create incentives for people not to reveal things that didn't go according to plan, further creating blind spots and failing to help the organization improve on a continuous basis.

Imagine, in contrast, a situation in which you as a leader make it clear that you expect people to try new things and that many of those may not work out (provided they are inexpensive and intelligently planned, as I described above). One of my favorite stories in this regard was an executive who regularly asked his direct reports in performance reviews to "show me your scrap heap." What he meant by that was that he wanted to see what the person had tried out during the review period, and what had been learned, even if the efforts came to naught. This practice makes it clear that doing nothing was not a safe way to conduct one's career.

It may sound a tad counterintuitive to evaluate people based on what they didn't do, but there are ways to make this more concrete. Some companies measure and incent people for creating a book of business with a certain percentage of new elements in it. 3M for years famously incentivized its executives to have at least 25 percent new product introductions in their overall portfolio. Procter & Gamble, as I mentioned above, incentivized its executives to obtain at least 50 percent of their new ideas from outside the firm. Another way to establish whether your firm is falling victim to sins of omission is by benchmarking. You might study, for instance, how well your folks are doing relative to selected industry peers. If the category is growing at 25 percent and your piece of it is only growing at 10 percent, that's a pretty strong signal that on a relative basis, you are falling behind.

A very structured approach to studying alternative courses of action for the purpose of identifying whether an important omission was made is the "after action review," a structured post-mortem activity employed by the military and popularized in the book *Hope is Not a Method*.[13] Essentially, an after action review asks the questions, "what did we hope to achieve?" "what actually happened?" "why did it happen?" and "what will we do differently next time?" Such a review can be a profound way to accelerate learning from unexpected events and making the basis for future decisions more clear.

Build Diversity into your Planning Approach

Research has long found that leaders have a tendency to surround themselves with people who are similar in terms of socioeconomic status, age, and other attributes.[14] A lack of diversity, however, risks undermining what management thinker Ashby referred to as "requisite variety."[15] The requisite variety principle basically means that in order to respond to an environment that is turbulent, the organization needs to be able to muster a number of different responses. The greater the turbulence, the greater internal variety an organization will need to cope.

Different individuals will pay different amounts of attention to unexpected events, and will draw different conclusions from them. It's essential, therefore, to provide the decision-makers in your organization with contrasting points of view and with the permission to engage in spirited debate about what various events might mean. If everyone has the same view of what is important, what matters, and what might happen in the future, effective learning is likely to be inhibited. Consider, for instance, how one interview respondent explained the ineffective response of the newspaper business to the advent of the Internet:

> Why did the whole newspaper industry cave into the "free" moment? I have an opinion. I think the news industry was a bit of deer in the headlights. You need to roll back the clock 15 years. If you roll back the clock and think about what a newspaper CEO worried about every day, these were the costs of paper acquisition and distribution, and they also worried a lot about labor.

The industry was renowned for its labor challenges. As a CEO, you didn't worry so much about your editorial skills and intellectual capital. You didn't worry about your advertising strength, because you believed you knew how to do that. They thought they knew what their portfolio of concerns was. The reason they rose to the top of their ranks is that they managed those resources incredibly effectively. Then this exceptionally disruptive thing showed up and they were entirely blinded by it. So my storyline for newspaper industry is that they were like deer in the headlights. The smartest people on the planet in that sector froze.

In other words, the teams managing many newspapers over the past 15 years were trapped by the tyranny of their past competitive agendas and were not able to mobilize their resources rapidly enough to move to a new business model. Part of the explanation was surely learning from others' behavior (once one news organization decided to start giving away its content, others followed), but also a certain similarity in their operational repertoires.

In Closing

It is all too easy for organizations to create the conditions under which planning—rather than being a process that facilitates learning from unexpected events—actually inhibits it. Plans become rigid structures that lead entrepreneurs and venture leaders to persist despite evidence that they should be rethinking their approach; or to not pursue opportunities simply because they are so blinded by current activities that they don't see them.

This does not have to be the case. The hopeful message I would like to leave you with is that learning from the unexpected is not necessarily expensive or difficult, but it does require different practices than one would use if you were convinced you had all the answers.

NOTES

1. Christensen, C.M., S.D. Anthony, and E.A. Roth, *Seeing what's next? Using the theories of innovation to predict industry change.* 2004, Boston: Harvard Business School Press. xxxix, 312.
2. Senge, P.M., "The leader's new work: Building learning organizations," *Sloan Management Review,* 1990. *Fall:* 7–23.
3. Levitt, B. and J.G. March, "Organizational learning," *Annual Review of Sociology,* 1988. *14:* 319–340.
4. McGrath, R.G. and I.C. MacMillan, "Discovery driven planning," *Harvard Business Review,* 1995. *73*(4): 44–54.
5. Christensen, C.M. and M.E. Raynor, "Why hard-nosed executives should care about management theory," *Harvard Business Review,* 2003. *81*(9): 66–74.
6. Kelly, K., "New rules for the new economy: Twelve dependable principles for thriving in a turbulent world," *Wired Magazine,* September 1997.

7.   Sitkin, S.B., "Learning through failure: The strategy of small losses," in *Research in organizational behavior, 14,* ed. B.M. Staw and L.L. Cummings. 1992, Greenwich, CT: JAI Press. 231–266.

8.   Kahneman, D., P. Slovic, and A. Tversky, *Judgment under uncertainty: Heuristics and biases.* 1982, Cambridge and New York: Cambridge University Press. xiii, 555.

9.   McGrath, R.G., "Falling forward: Real options reasoning and entrepreneurial failure," *Academy of Management Review,* 1999. *24*(1): 13–30.

10. Warshaw, M., "The state of small business 2000," in *Inc. Magazine,* 2000: 15–16.

11. Moon, Y., *IKEA invades America.* 2004, Boston: Harvard Business School Publishing.

12. Kirby, J. and T.A. Stewart, "The institutional yes: Interview with Jeff Bezos of Amazon.com." *Harvard Business Review,* 2007. *85*(10): 75–82.

13. Sullivan, G.R. and M.V. Harper, *Hope is not a method: What business leaders can learn from America's army.* 1997, New York: Broadway Books.

14. Hambrick, D. and P. Mason, "Upper echelons: The organization as a reflection of its top managers," *Academy of Management Review,* 1984. *9*(3): 193–206.

15. Ashby, W.R., *An introduction to cybernetics.* 1956, London: Chapman and Hall.

Chapter 4

Evidence-Based Management for Entrepreneurial Environments: Faster and Better Decisions with Less Risk

JEFFREY PFEFFER

ENTREPRENEURSHIP IS RISKY. Most new technologies and new businesses fail. Shane (2008) reported that 25 percent of new businesses failed in the first year and that by the fifth year, fewer than half had survived. In the United Kingdom, Stark (2001) presented data showing a 75 percent failure rate for small and medium-sized enterprises in the first three years. The risk and high failure rate is because most new ideas and technologies are not good and are, therefore, rejected by the marketplace.

High failure rates have become accepted as an inevitable cost of entrepreneurial activity, offset by the jobs, wealth, and ideas created by those new ventures that are successful. So the venture capital industry's business model is premised on getting a few exceptional returns ("home runs") among the multitude of failures in each portfolio. For instance, a German venture capital fund begun in the late 1990s showed a cumulative internal rate of return of negative 3.8 percent as of 2009, almost break-even over the period. But of the 28 investments the fund had made, 11 had no value at all and four were worth less than 15 percent of the value of the initial investment. The almost break-even return was the result of one investment worth four times and another six times the amount invested as well as some smaller positive returns. A study of 128 exited investments in the United Kingdom also reported a highly skewed distribution of returns, with 34 percent being a total loss, 13 percent of the exits at break-even or a partial loss, and 23 percent of the investments having an internal rate of return of above 50 percent (Mason and Harrison 2002).

As a consequence of this high rate of failure for new ventures, both human and financial resources go to waste. Many talented people, including engineers, scientists, and others with advanced degrees spend enormous time and energy on entrepreneurial activities with little to show for it other than what they learned from the experience. The wasted effort derives in part from the fact that it is often difficult to know when a new venture is beyond hope or when the investment of a little more time and money can make it successful. There are numerous examples, the Apple Newton being just one, of a product idea that failed because it was too early for the market, where subsequent variations of the same basic idea turn out to be huge commercial successes. Consequently, the temptation to persist is strong. Such persistence reflects the psychology of escalating commitment (e.g. Staw 1976), which argues that people do not want to admit they have made a mistake with the negative implications for their self-concept and therefore become psychologically identified with their decisions. This persistence also reflects the uncertainty of not knowing when a small incremental investment will actually make the earlier efforts pay off (Heath 1995). And there is a natural tendency to not quit and consequently risk having others capitalize on the unrealized potential of one's efforts. If it were possible to more quickly and accurately forecast the likelihood of success and make decisions that would increase success rates, at least some of that human capital would not go to waste.

A similar waste of resources characterizes the financial capital that is plowed into entrepreneurial ventures. The evidence shows that many investors do not earn returns commensurate with the risks they take. Kaplan and Schoar examined returns to private equity—venture capital and leveraged buyout funds—over the period 1980–2001. They found that the median internal rate of return for VC funds was 11 percent and that the median venture capital fund's performance was only about two-thirds that of the public market equivalent, measured as the return to the Standard & Poor's 500 (Kaplan and Schoar 2005). Cochrane (2005), looking at individual transactions rather than funds, a methodology that admittedly leaves out management and performance fees accruing to the general partner, concluded that VC returns were similar, in their means, standard deviations, and volatility, to the returns shown by smaller NASDAQ-traded stocks. However, lacking a public market, the venture capital investments were inherently riskier and less liquid.

Industry-wide estimates of financial returns to entrepreneurial investments are highly skewed by a few prominent, early and successful entrants to the venture capital and for that matter the hedge fund industry that have earned exceptional returns. Kaplan and Schoar (2005) noted the substantial heterogeneity in returns to venture capital funds. Indeed, one manager of a fund of funds investing in other venture capital partnerships commented that more than 100 percent of the industry's returns were earned by the top 20 (in terms of performance) firms, which means that there are literally hundreds of venture capital firms that have returned nothing to their investors.

These poor results from much, although obviously not all, entrepreneurial activity occur in spite of the hard work and diligence of many talented individuals. Moreover, little seems to have changed over time, indicating that there has been little learning or improvement in decision-making quality. These facts suggest that there may be potential to improve the decision-making process associated with developing and building new enterprises.

WHY HIGH FAILURE RATES FOR ENTREPRENEURSHIP PERSIST

There are several causes for the persistently high failure rates for new businesses. One problem is that it has become conventional wisdom, accepted by all the parties ranging from entrepreneurs to those who provide them with financing, that a high rate of failure is an inevitable consequence of doing new things, inventing new technologies, and opening up new markets—activities which are inherently risky and uncertain because they involve doing things that have not been successfully done before. Because this conventional wisdom suggests that a high failure rate is inevitable, there is often little effort expended trying to improve decision-making in new venture activity.

A tremendous amount of the culture of high technology entrepreneurship is carried in and influenced by the venture capital community. Many of these firms do what they do without much introspection or reflection, partly as a result of the egos and self-confidence of the VC partners. One of the more consistent findings in social psychology is the so-called "above-average effect," in which more than half of most people believe they are above average on virtually all positive qualities, even including height and income (see, for instance, Kruger 1999; Chambers and Windschitl 2004). People who have survived and prospered in the venture industry have obviously done well, and those VCs who don't do well generally don't last. Therefore, it is axiomatic that most fund managers believe they are much above average in their abilities and in their decision-making. Consequently, many believe they don't need to learn much or have much to learn. This attitude exists even though VC success may be as much a function of the particular firm where one works, one's timing in both entering the industry and when investments were made, and random good luck as a consequence of any particular individual skill. There is much research that suggests that when good performance outcomes occur, positive qualities get attributed to the people, groups, or companies that enjoy those good outcomes (e.g. Staw 1975; Rosenzweig 2007). This association of positive attributes with good performance occurs whether or not such attributes were causally related to the good results or even whether or not the high-performing entities actually possess the positive qualities. This means that high-performing VCs will be perceived as having individual skill as a consequence of their performance, whether or not such skill actually exists.

Precedent and the way things are done in the entrepreneurial financing industry have been substitutes for thinking for quite a while (Pfeffer and Sutton 1980). Yet another issue that constrains improvement in decision-making is that pressures to do what others in the industry are doing, because of the assumption that the crowd is invariably wise, are strong. Entrepreneurs, too, mostly have strong egos, which is what is required to take on something new where the risks of failure are high. But this overconfidence among entrepreneurs and those that back them makes it difficult for people involved in creating new businesses to question things and to learn from setbacks and other experience.

Moreover, most venture capitalists and entrepreneurs believe that outstanding individual people make the difference, leading them to focus on finding and recruiting stars and to eschew much attention to process, including decision-making processes. In addition, most investors engage in a set of ritualized due diligence practices with little effort to close the loop and learn from the results of their decisions—after-action or after-event reviews are reasonably rare. With little effort expended to improve entrepreneurial decision quality, not surprisingly, decision quality doesn't improve. Therefore, failure rates don't change. This persistence of failure rates over time seemingly reinforces the validity of the conventional wisdom that high failure is an inevitable consequence of entrepreneurial activity. And the cycle continues.

Yet another possible reason for such small changes in rates of failure is that few of the participants in entrepreneurial activity suffer significant consequences from unsuccessful decisions, and therefore many players have less incentive than one might expect to improve their decision-making. As has been documented, much of the return to the principals or general partners in both hedge funds and venture capital funds comes from the guaranteed annual percentage they earn, typically 2 percent of the amount of the fund's principal (Mackintosh 2009). Entrepreneurs often, although not always, are working with other people's money, so their financial downside, except in terms of the opportunity costs of their time, are also limited. And, because failure is most often seen as an unavoidable risk of being an entrepreneur, there are few if any career risks for starting something that doesn't work out. Many entrepreneurs go on to work at least temporarily in VC firms and few have much difficulty finding subsequent jobs or, for that matter, investment capital. John Lilly, for instance, currently the CEO of the Internet browser company Mozilla, was first the CEO of Reactivity, a company that was ultimately unsuccessful.

I am unconvinced that high rates of failure are inevitable and that improvement in decision-making is impossible. Consequently, in this chapter, I outline a case for applying evidence-based management to entrepreneurial activity. After first defining the elements of an evidence-based management approach, I consider a few commonly voiced but largely inaccurate objections to its use and then provide some examples of how evidence-based decision-making has been and could be used to improve the quality of entrepreneurial decision-making. My argument is premised on the idea that people can improve the quality of their decision-making in all environments, and that an evidence-based approach is one reasonable way to accomplish this.

THE FOUNDATIONS OF EVIDENCE-BASED MANAGEMENT

Evidence-based management (hereafter EBM) is modeled on the evidence-based movement in medical practice. Although evidence-based decision-making in medicine is growing in its acceptance, in medicine as well as in other contexts such as criminology and education, evidence-based practice has historically faced resistance to its implementation. That resistance continues to the present (Domurad 2005) and makes implementing evidence-based management more challenging than it should be.

EBM seeks to apply the best currently available data and theory to managerial decision-making (Pfeffer and Sutton 2006). The underlying assumption is that although it is the case that at any given point in time information is incomplete and over time the evidence on what to do and how to do it changes as new data come in, in general, decision quality will be higher if people make fact-based decisions. Moreover, it is incumbent on both individual organizations and larger communities of practice to systematically gather and learn from actual experience so that, over time, decision quality progressively improves. EBM emphasizes gathering and paying attention to the data, understanding the best current theory about the subject of a particular decision, and continually updating both theory and evidence as new information becomes available. Although such an approach seems logical and, indeed, almost like common sense, it actually requires a different mindset than is common in most organizational management.

As we know, decisions are not always based on data and theory (Pfeffer and Sutton 2006). Instead, organizations frequently rely on casual benchmarking—following what others are doing regardless of whether the experience of others in possibly quite different circumstances is relevant to their own case. Leaders also make decisions based on their own experience, even though such experience is often unreliable as a guide for subsequent action for several reasons. Experience is a problematic guide to action because there is a tendency to see what we expect to see, the basis of all magic acts, which means learning from experience is difficult and requires effort. Few organizations outside of the military, with its after-event or after-action reviews and medicine, with its mortality and morbidity conferences, engage in the systematic, structured reflection that would be required to learn from experience. Experience is also inherently idiosyncratic, reflecting a particular case and set of circumstances, and therefore suffers as a guide to action from the problem of trying to derive general principles from very small samples. Finally, experience at its best is a guide for decision-making in situations that mirror the past from which the experience comes, but past experience may be unreliable in providing guidance in very different or novel contexts.

In addition to experience, decisions often reflect what leaders believe to be true—their ideology (Tetlock 2000)—and what they have done in the past and seems to have worked. Ideology colors what people see and how they apprehend the world around them, as well as how they incorporate their observations into decisions. As such, ideology, and by this I mean political ideology, colors what people do even in business decision contexts (Tetlock 2000). In addition, people naturally tend to advocate doing things that favor their own competencies and interests and that are consistent with enhancing their self-image. None of these bases for making decisions leads to particularly sound, fact-based choices.

With its emphasis on taking action on the basis of the best knowledge available at the moment while recognizing that all knowledge is imperfect and therefore we need to learn from experience, evidence-based management is consistent in its underlying philosophy with an attitude of wisdom. As psychologists John Meacham and Robert Sternberg have argued, wisdom means knowing what you know and what you don't know, and acting on the basis of what is known at the moment while being open to changing your mind (e.g. Meacham 1983; Sternberg 1985).

With the emphasis on data and feedback processes, EBM is also consistent with the principles of design thinking as practiced in places like product design company IDEO and other firms such as Procter & Gamble (e.g. Kelley 2001; Brown 2008; Martin 2009). A design-oriented approach emphasizes prototyping and systematically learning from experience and also getting into the field to see how real people actually use products and services so that new versions can be based on the issues people face as they interact with the company's products. EBM is quite consistent with this notion of running experiments—building prototypes and seeing how people react—and also with embedding design in learning from real situations.

Finally, the evidence-based management idea is also consistent with many of the ideas of the total quality movement. Just as in the case of quality efforts, EBM stresses diagnosing the root causes of problems and addressing those fundamental sources rather than just treating symptoms or acting without doing any diagnosis at all. Also, like the quality movement, EBM emphasizes the gathering of systematic data to the extent possible so that actions can be formulated using the best information available.

The quality movement and its approach has fallen into some disuse—even Toyota has recently experienced substantial product problems—mostly because an emphasis on quality requires systematic, persistent discipline that is difficult to maintain when confronted by the temptation to try new ideas and the boredom and fatigue that results from close attention to detail and process. And although design thinking has been featured in numerous books and articles, it, too, is not as widely practiced as its apparent publicity success would suggest.

OBJECTIONS TO AN EVIDENCE-BASED MANAGEMENT APPROACH

If evidence-based management and other, complementary approaches are not widely used, it is important to understand why. We frequently hear the same issues raised as objections to using evidence-based management, and some of these concerns would seem particularly relevant for entrepreneurial decision-making. One concern is that the current business environment changes more rapidly than in the past, and the high velocity of competitive dynamics makes any process that takes a long time virtually irrelevant. Because it relies on facts, theory, and analysis, evidence-based decision-making takes more time than just acting on gut instinct or recalled experience. A second, related issue is that there are many decision circumstances for which good evidence and theory simply do not exist, rendering EBM largely moot. This would seem to be particularly the case for entrepreneurial decisions. What data or evidence can possibly be brought to bear on decisions about launching new technologies and new products into a competitive environment fraught with uncertainty? If entrepreneurs have succeeded in the past against all odds on the basis of their persistence, sometimes in the face of evidence that would argue against what they had done, this success only convinces them to ignore data, particularly data contrary to their intuitions, in the future. This often-misguided reliance in their own intuition occurs because history is often ambiguous and organizational learning is a process fraught with difficulties (e.g. Levitt and March 1988; Levinthal and March 1993).

Third, very much as is the case with evidence-based medicine, executives are extremely reluctant to substitute theory or data for their own personal clinical experience and judgment. This latter point helps explain why there is so little transfer of knowledge between the research and practitioner domains of management.

None of these issues seems particularly compelling and there are things to be done in any event to mitigate their relevance. Even though many leaders complain about the length of time ostensibly required to implement evidence-based decision-making, many of these same leaders, even those in relatively small, high-technology enterprises, seem perfectly content to hire management consulting firms to provide advice and executive search firms to go outside to find additional talent. Such engagements typically not only cost a great deal of money, they often take months to complete and in the case of executive search, often result in either no hire or a poor one.

Practicing evidence-based management need not consume a lot of time in any event. With online databases and libraries that cover virtually every conceivable question, searching for the best theory and data takes comparatively little effort. Google Scholar is one such site that brings relevant research from peer-reviewed academic journals to a person's fingertips. Although not all of the content found on that site is free, the cost for accessing most articles is modest and pales in comparison to the consequences of the decisions companies make. And there is much information about products, services, company financial results, and markets available for a modest amount of effort or cost.

Often applying evidence-based management thinking is simply a matter of uncovering the assumptions that underlie some potential choice and then accessing the collective wisdom of one's colleagues to see whether or not those assumptions seem sensible. If the assumptions underlying a particular intervention don't seem plausible, then the odds of that intervention succeeding are remote.

As one example of this process in action, consider the decision to implement forced-curve performance ranking, something advocated by Jack Welch, the former CEO of General Electric, among others, and a practice that is widely implemented in companies of all sizes (e.g. Novations Group 2004). Although there is actually a great deal of research on the effects of forced-curve ranking systems under different business circumstances such as the degree of interdependence among tasks, the frequency of feedback, and what happens to low and high performers (e.g. Blume et al. 2009), one doesn't actually need to even access that evidence to ascertain whether or not implementing a forced-curve ranking system will be helpful. That's because like all organizational interventions, this management practice has embedded within it a set of implicit assumptions about employees, managers, and organizational effectiveness. Some of those assumptions in the case of forced-curve ranking systems are: people can be objectively ranked against each other; people will respond positively with efforts to improve their performance when they know their position in the rankings; managers will provide objective and reasonably frequent feedback to their employees telling them where they stand; and the competitive dynamics that are an inherent property of systems that cause people to compete with each other will not adversely affect learning or organizational performance. Although such assumptions may be true in some cases, in general they probably do not hold—which is why there is little evidence that forced-curve ranking improves performance and some evidence that suggests that this management practice causes numerous problems (Novations Group 2004).

In addition to uncovering assumptions, companies can move to better capture and utilize the data they gather as a result of their ongoing activities. Even relatively small companies today gather lots of data as part of their operations, information ranging from sales to customer complaints and returns to product development time to data on turnover and employee recruitment. Information-gathering is more automated and the cost of computer memory has fallen to trivial levels. Although there is much data on operations and sales, often such data are used primarily for accounting purposes or in organizational subunits such as operations or human resources, but they are not brought together at the senior level to provide a foundation for comprehensive, data-based strategic action. This is not just a problem in small, new enterprises—David Larcker, an accounting professor at Stanford, has shared numerous examples of larger companies that do not understand the process by which they make money in that they don't know their most profitable customers or even products and often have inaccurate estimates of costs.

Finally, entrepreneurs and their funders would be well served to recognize the inherent difficulties and biases in estimating their degree of expertise and in over-learning the apparent importance of persistence in the face of seemingly contradictory evidence about the prospects for success. Business success is inherently an uncertain process. The point of EBM, much like its counterparts in medicine and the policy sciences, is not to perfectly account for every single instance, but rather, by the systematic application of data and theory, improve the odds of making a better decision.

HOW THINGS MIGHT BE DIFFERENT: EVIDENCE-BASED MANAGEMENT IN SMALL ENTREPRENEURIAL COMPANIES

Businesses founded on or using the Internet automatically generate a great deal of data. These data have traditionally been used mostly for analyzing and designing marketing campaigns and, of course, for assessing the effectiveness of various advertising strategies. But it is possible to use such data to build truly evidence-based companies, and the model offered by some of these enterprises provides ideas that can be employed by any organization or start-up, not just those doing software development or focused on the Internet.

Because of the high failure rate and its associated waste of resources, recently, some venture capitalists—although not necessarily the largest or most well known—and some software companies have begun to advocate a different way of doing business and managing. Sometimes called agile software development, the movement began in the software space particularly for products oriented to the web. But the movement—which is what this set of ideas should be called since it has advocates and seeks to change how companies do their business—seems to be diffusing. Based on the "lean" principles of Toyota, the idea is to expend as few resources as possible while you learn what the customer wants from your product or service, doing rapid iterations of new releases—putting the rapid prototyping ideas from new product development into action. Because learning is an explicit goal, agile development and lean design necessitates gathering and analyzing information so that every new iteration can incorporate past experience as efficiently and effectively as possible.

One articulation of the idea of quickly learning from experience comes from the book and website, *Getting Real.* As the company behind the book and the website, 37 Signals, explains it:

- Getting Real is about skipping all the stuff that represents real (charts, graphs, boxes, arrows, schematics, wireframes, etc.) and actually building the real thing.
- Getting Real is less. Less mass, less software, less features, less paperwork, less of everything that's not essential . . .
- Getting Real is staying small and being agile.
- Getting Real starts with the interface, the real screens that people are going to use. It begins with what the customer actually experiences and builds backwards from there. This lets you get the interface right before you get the software wrong.
- Getting Real is about iterations and lowering the cost of change. Getting Real is all about launching, tweaking, and constantly improving (37 Signals 2010).

Traditional software or, for that matter, almost any traditional product develop-ment process proceeds following what is sometimes called a waterfall or cascade process. First, an engineer or marketing person comes up with a product idea or change to an existing product. The product is then designed, often by engineers, and specifications developed. A prototype is made, and if it is a physical product, a bill of materials gets created and a manufacturing process is designed. If it is a software product, code gets written. Then the product goes through quality assurance to ensure compliance with the original design specifications, after which it is released to the market. At that point, marketing and sales tries to promote and sell something that has already been created, often with little to no end-user input.

Note that this traditional product or service development process takes a long time and entails significant investment *before* the company receives *any* market feedback. The agile process aims to short circuit this delay and cut the amount of investment by getting customer input early in the process and engaging in rapid, low-cost product iterations, in each instance gathering data and learning as much as possible from such data.

One example of a company that assiduously adheres to an evidence-based management, agile approach is Rypple. Founded by some former senior leaders from the workforce scheduling company, Workbrain, Rypple's aim was to overcome many of the limitations of the traditional performance management process. Although people want to improve and desire feedback, the traditional, hierarchical appraisal process, often tied to monetary compensation, sometimes requiring ranking people against each other, is almost universally disliked. Employees do not like getting appraisals and few managers enjoy doing them. Rypple's goal was to design a software system that made asking for and providing feedback anonymous, quick, and easy.

The company and its culture are very data driven. Even as a very small start-up, they hired an MIT business school graduate whose mission was data and analytics. And every step of the way, Rypple emphasized gathering information, learning from it, and then improving the product as well as the distribution process.

Daniel Debow, co-CEO and co-founder, noted that instead of thinking in terms of a "product launch cycle," it was more useful to think of a "customer discovery cycle." Right from the beginning, Rypple's people had the objective of not proving themselves right, but instead, proving themselves wrong, and along the way, to have humility in their inability to accurately predict the future. In the beginning, they built just paper (PowerPoint) prototypes of the Rypple product. As Debow noted, "before we even hired a developer, we just built PowerPoint mock-ups and put them in front of people to see how they would react." Based on potential user interest and comments, the company then built a very bare prototype—no security, for instance, or log-in. They showed this prototype to some more people who wanted to use it, so Rypple put this bare-bones prototype into a couple of companies to see what happened. Based on that initial user feedback, the cycle of iteration and learning continued.

Rypple could and did continuously gather data on how many people were using the various prototypes, how many people were responding to requests for feedback, what ways of requesting feedback generated the most and best responses, what the pattern of usage was, and so forth. They tweaked phrasing, the user interface design, every aspect of the service, and carefully monitored variations in user response. Over time, other features such as security were added. But the cycle time for new iterations was almost weekly, and the cycle time for learning and incorporating that learning into new generations of the product were just about as fast.

One of the reasons Rypple could "afford" to have its users help develop the product without upsetting those people is because the initial version of the product, not for companies but for individuals, was free. If people haven't committed money to some licensed software, they are less irritated if the product isn't perfect. And because of the agile and lean software development process, Rypple didn't need to generate as much money because its expenditures on the typical product development process had been drastically reduced—not only in resources but in time.

Debow was quite clear as to why he had not been able to implement a similar process in Workbrain and why there was resistance to a data-driven development cycle in many traditional companies: control. As he told me:

> Everybody in software had been brought up on the rational IBM-like products
> and these very engineering-oriented processes and documentation. That was
> the way people were going to control for bugs or other issues and get things

right. It was all about control. What is at the core of a lot of this agile and lean thinking is that actually you can't claim anything. And that kind of killed people.

The lean movement in software development requires, everyone agrees, more than just analytics expertise. It entails an enormous mindset shift, about how a company does product development, about the amount of control exercised at each stage of the process, about listening to customers, about the role and treatment of employees, about the importance of speed—and most importantly, about being committed to hearing the truth, whatever that truth is. That is the biggest barrier to implementing evidence-based management: the shift required in how leaders think about their job and the process of getting work done. This is a barrier that exists in large, traditional companies but also persists in small, entrepreneurial ventures. Overcoming the traditional mindsets can, as in the case of agile software development, lower risk by getting better market data more quickly and lower the waste of resources through a leaner, more efficient process. As such, this evidence-based approach can provide a competitive advantage, but only to those people with the wisdom to use it.

CONCLUSION

Two things seem to be true. First, evidence-based management could improve entrepreneurial decision-making, reducing risks, costs, and wasted time and effort—just as an evidence-based approach could benefit most if not all organizations and just as evidence-based medicine has improved medical practice and outcomes while saving money. Second, the mindset shift required to implement EBM is apparently large. Therefore, evidence-based approaches struggle even when they could demonstrably save vast sums of money and even lives.

But as the recent history of the lean or agile software movement illustrates, the competitive advantages from listening to the data are substantial. And in the end, much like medicine and various branches of public policy, particularly in countries other than the United States, the implementation of an evidence-based approach will gain traction. It is just a matter of time. In the meantime, however, those entrepreneurs and suppliers of risk capital who avail themselves of evidence-based thinking will be in a much stronger competitive position.

REFERENCES

Blume, Brian D., Baldwin, Timothy T., and Rubin, Robert S. (2009) "Reactions to Different Types of Forced Distribution Performance Evaluation Systems," *Journal of Business and Psychology*, 24: 77–91.

Brown, Tim (2008) "Design Thinking," *Harvard Business Review*, 86 (June): 84–92.

Chambers, John R. and Windschitl, Paul D. (2004) "Biases in Social Comparative Judgments: The Role of Nonmotivated Factors in Above-average and Comparative-optimism Effects," *Psychological Bulletin*, 130: 813–838.

Cochrane, John H. (2005) "The Risk and Return of Venture Capital," *Journal of Financial Economics*, 75: 3–52.

Domurad, Frank (2005) "Doing Evidence-based Policy and Practices ain't for Sissies," *Community Corrections Report on Law and Corrections Practice*, 12: 49–50ff.

Heath, Chip (1995) "Escalation and *De*-escalation of Commitment in Response to Sunk Costs: The Role of Budgeting in Mental Accounting," *Organizational Behavior and Human Decision Processes*, 62: 38–54.

Kaplan, Steven N. and Schoar, Antoinette (2005) "Private Equity Performance: Returns, Persistence, and Capital Flows," *Journal of Finance*, 60: 1791–1823.

Kelley, Tom (2001) *The Art of Innovation*. New York: Currency.

Kruger, Justin (1999) "Lake Wobegon be Gone! The 'Below-Average Effect' and the Egocentric Nature of Comparative Ability Judgments," *Journal of Personality and Social Psychology*, 77: 221–232.

Levinthal, Daniel A. and March, James G. (1993) "The Myopia of Learning," *Strategic Management Journal*, 14: 95–112.

Levitt, Barbara and March, James G. (1988) "Organizational Learning," *Annual Review of Sociology*, 14: 319–340.

Mackintosh, James (2009) "Hedge Fund Investors Have a Great Chance to Cut Fees," Ft.com, February 6.

Martin, Roger (2009) *The Design of Business*. Boston: Harvard Business Press.

Mason, Colin M. and Harrison, Richard T. (2002) "Is it Worth it? The Rates of Return from Informal Venture Capital Investments," *Journal of Business Venturing*, 17: 211–236.

Meacham, John A. (1983) "Wisdom and the Context of Knowledge: Knowing What One Doesn't Know One Doesn't Know," in D. Huhn and J. A. Meacham (Eds.), *On The Development of Developmental Psychology*. Basel: Krager, 111–134.

Novations Group (2004) "Uncovering the growing disenchantment with forced ranking performance management systems." Boston: Novations Group, White Paper.

Pfeffer, Jeffrey and Sutton, Robert I. (1980) *The Knowing–Doing Gap: How Smart Companies Turn Knowledge into Action*. Boston: Harvard Business School Press.

Pfeffer, Jeffrey and Sutton, Robert I. (2006) *Hard Facts, Dangerous Half-truths, and Total Nonsense: Profiting from Evidence-based Management*. Boston: Harvard Business School Press.

Rosenzweig, Phil (2007) *The Halo Effect*. New York: Free Press.

Shane, Scott (2008) Startup failure rates—the REAL numbers. Available at: http://small biztrends.com/2008/04/startup-failure-rates.html.

Stark, Antony (2001) SME support in Britain. Available at: www.adb.org/Documents/Reports/PRC-SME/App5-UK.pdf.

Staw, Barry M. (1975) "Attribution of the 'Causes' of Performance: A General Alternative Interpretation of Cross-sectional Research on Organizations," *Organizational Behavior and Human Performance*, 13: 414–432.

Staw, Barry M. (1976) "Knee Deep in the Big Muddy: A Study of Escalating Commitment to a Chosen Course of Action," *Organizational Behavior and Human Performance*, 16: 27–44.

Sternberg, Robert J. (1985) "Implicit Theories of Intelligence, Creativity, and Wisdom," *Journal of Personality and Social Psychology*, 49: 607–627.

Tetlock, Phillip E. (2000) "Cognitive Biases and Organizational Correctives: Do Both Disease and Cure Depend on the Politics of the Beholder?" *Administrative Science Quarterly*, 46: 293–326.

Chapter 5

Betting the Farm: Real Options, Scenario Analysis, and Strategic Reasoning about Risk

DAVID L. BODDE

If you can make one heap of all your winnings
And risk it on one turn of pitch-and-toss,
And lose, and start again at your beginnings
And never breathe a word about your loss . . .
Then you'll face indictment for financial sinnings
And owe an explanation to your boss.

With apologies to Rudyard Kipling

PLACING BIG BETS might be a test of manhood when risking your own money, but when you are risking the fortunes of others, it becomes a recipe for disaster. For new, technology-based ventures, two characteristics can lead corporate innovators, entrepreneurs, and investors into accepting such large-scale risks. The first is a characteristic of the business environment surrounding the project: the external conditions having greatest influence over the success of the venture are highly volatile and defy any reasonable understanding, let alone forecast. This is the domain of "ignorance" discussed in the Introduction to Part II. The second derives from the nature of the venture itself. Consider an important subset of technology ventures— for example, any kind of advanced energy project like an offshore oil drilling platform or a coal-fired power plant; a private spacecraft like that pioneered by Virgin Galactic; an electric powertrain automobile; and so forth. The functional characteristics of many such ventures include:

- Immediacy. A prompt decision must be made to pursue an opportunity or to pass it up. The conditions for success now appear favorable, but once the opportunity has passed, there can be no guarantee that these favorable conditions will return.

- Capital Risk. The venture requires a large upfront investment, most of which must be committed before the value from the project can be achieved.
- Duration of Exposure. Radical changes in the business environment can affect the risk exposure of this investment for a protracted period, perhaps as much as 30 years. Such disruptive changes can include: advances in rival technologies; regulatory and legislated requirements; resource abundance or scarcity; currency exchange rates; and the like.

Little can be done to reduce the situational difficulties arising from this kind of venture, but entrepreneurs and innovators can reduce the risks they pose through two guides to strategic thinking: real options reasoning, which values a risky project by the flexibility it creates; and scenario-based analysis of the business environment, which illuminates the options that offer greatest value in alternative futures. Though often treated as distinct and separate tools, their use in combination multiplies their power to manage strategic risk.

REAL OPTIONS: THE VALUE OF FLEXIBILITY

Think of any option as a *contingent decision*. In exchange for some upfront cost, the decision-maker gains the ability to defer action until the passage of time reveals new information. The value of the flexibility gained must, of course, exceed the price required to secure the option. In the case of real options, the postponed decision most often concerns commitment to a project whose success turns on highly uncertain events over which the company or entrepreneur has little control[1]—the kind of decision described above. Practice has given rise to a rich variety of real options, which allow the innovator to invest in discrete stages, employ alternative inputs or locations, grow capacity faster or slower, or even to abandon the project entirely. This adaptability has led some researchers to view real options as generators of strategic choice (Bowman and Hurry 1993).

The underlying logic of real options builds from the well-known financial options, which offer the holder the ability, but not the obligation, to purchase or sell a security (say, a common stock) at a predetermined price. Financial options can be purchased in public markets and remain in effect for a specified period. If an option expires ``out of the money'' and hence is unused, then its holder loses no more than the price of its purchase.

Three conditions combine to govern the value and use of financial options (Adner and Levinthal 2004):

- The value of the underlying financial asset, and hence the value of the option, depends on events beyond the investor's control. No amount of cleverness (the legal kind, anyway) on the part of the option's purchaser can influence this value.
- An open marketplace provides unambiguous signals of the option's value, again independent of the actions of investors.
- The option investor's choices are limited to exercising the option or abandoning it to expire valueless at the end of its term.

The precision and ease of replication that follows from these conditions has enabled financial researchers to develop elaborate quantitative methods for their valuation, thus making financial options valuable in hedged investment strategies. But we should not suppose that strict adherence is desirable, or even possible, in the world of real options (McGrath et al. 2004).

Like its financial counterpart, a real option allows the holder to choose a course of action after an unknowable future reveals more of its hazards and opportunities. Beyond that, however, the strict conditions necessary for valuing hedged financial bets are not relevant to real options. Indeed, the real options have value precisely because they enable active management, the flexibility to change strategic direction as circumstances warrant. Further, real options recognize the path-dependent nature of most technology investments: the value of reaching a later stage in a sequential development process depends on what was learned in the prior stages. And finally, real options reasoning facilitates organizational learning by providing a documentable framework that specifies the expectations for success or failure in advance. Learning becomes possible when these expectations are compared with reality, even at the cost of some embarrassment. Thus, real options improve the decision-making process as well as contribute new inputs to those decisions.

At the tactical level, real options analysis (a quantification of real options reasoning) enables entrepreneurs and innovators to overcome two key limitations of discounted cash flow (DCF) analysis, the most widely used tool for estimating the value of a risky project. The first limitation arises from rigidity: DCF analysis presumes that the cash flows can indeed be specified over the life of the project and that the originally chosen discount rate remains appropriate. The second limitation reinforces the first. Innovators can make their projects look attractive in competition with others by minimizing cash outlays. Too often, these very lean projects lack the flexibility needed to respond to highly volatile circumstances—the domain of "ignorance" where one can neither identify the hazardous events nor estimate their likelihood. Hence, the venture's vulnerability to these events can even increase in a DCF-managed environment.

Many excellent references can guide entrepreneurs and innovators in creating and valuing real options, both at the strategic and tactical levels (Amram and Kulatilaka 1999; Trigeorgis 2000). It is not our intent to replicate these here but instead to illuminate the power of real options thinking in managing risk. Consider a simple illustration of the strategic use of real options: a hypothetical new venture that by early 2011 was in a position to enter the electric vehicle market as early as 2013 with a battery electric automobile. We will call it (unimaginatively) EV Venture. Achieving the 2013 entry date would require a large investment in production facilities and a simultaneous, but smaller, investment in research for product development.

Alternatively, EV Venture could defer the production facilities for a year while completing the product development campaign. That would defer the production decision but allow a market launch by 2015. This alternative, a real option (albeit highly simplified), retains for the new venture the capability to ramp up production for market entry, but does not create the obligation to do so: the classic case of a limited commitment that creates future decision rights. The price the company would pay is delayed entry into an already thin market.

To choose wisely, the new venture's management team must consider: (a) risks from the reactions of competitors; and (b) risks from the business environment, chiefly volatility in the price of petroleum and the vagaries of political support for electric vehicles. These risks illustrate how real options combined with other analytic methods can offer greater understanding than either could in isolation.

COMPETITOR RISK: REAL OPTIONS AND GAME THEORY

Most analysts consider the near-term EV market a specialized niche focused on urban environments where: (a) the EV directly addresses congestion and pollution concerns; (b) smaller size offers an advantage, not an issue; (c) a greater density of recharging opportunities can be provided; and (d) a more affluent customer base is concentrated. By early 2011, several EV companies were already competing in this market including new ventures like Aptera Motors, Miles Electric Vehicles, Tesla Motors, and the infelicitously named Zap Electric Vehicles. In addition, service-based business models like Zip-Car or car2go[2] were offering urban consumers affordable, personal transportation without having to own the vehicle. Most importantly, by 2011 global automakers like Nissan already had electric vehicles in the marketplace, and others like GM and BMW had announced strategic initiatives in electric vehicles for urban use.

A tipping point will eventually catapult the EV into the mainstream, perhaps as early as 2020 (Ernst & Young 2010). But well before the mainstream marketplace welcomes the EV, the actions of these competitors can strongly influence the profitability, market share, and survival of EV Venture. And so, its management team will need to identify from the general set above those competitors most able to influence their success. Once these competitors are identified, then "option games" can contribute to strategic reasoning with real options.

Game theory, a term that calls to mind images of mildly loony academics scribbling on equation-filled blackboards, can supplement real options analysis by adding explicit consideration of competitor moves. For EV Venture, four basic scenarios span the range of possibilities: (1) all relevant competitors including EV Venture invest immediately in manufacturing; (2) none of them invests immediately; (3) EV Venture invests immediately, but its chief competitors defer; and (4) the competitors invest but EV Venture defers (Ferreira et al. 2009). The market consequences of each of these possibilities can then be estimated together with a subjective assessment of the likelihood that they will occur.

The resulting decision tree has the effect of organizing the subjective assessments made by the EV Venture management team in seeking to estimate the value of the year's delay. Figure 5.1 illustrates how this can be done to assess the implications of competitor response in the event that EV Venture should defer a production commitment from now (T1) until the future (T2). The strategic considerations in

Real options reasoning allows EV Venture to assess the risks and value of making a small investment now (T1) to continue technology development while deferring the big bet on new production capacity until (T2)

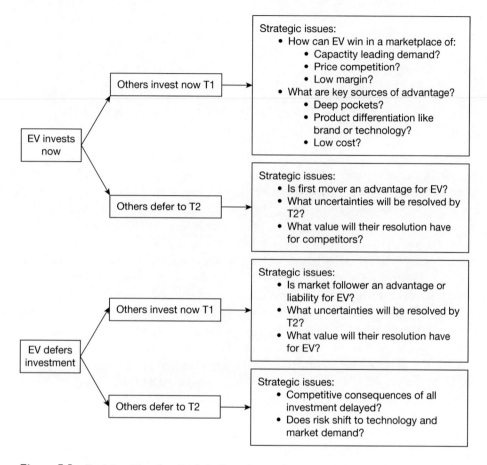

Figure 5.1. Decision Tree for Real Options Reasoning

boxes on the far right of Figure 5.1 would then frame EV Venture's reasoning about the likelihood of competitor responses and the consequences of each.

Much has been written about methods for quantifying these decision trees (see Grenadier 2000 or Rogers 2009), but the inherent subjectivity of the underlying estimates of consequence and likelihood remains. As a practical matter, the quantitative results best serve to illustrate the value of a real option under varying circumstances. But when decision-makers rely excessively on quantitative estimates to prescribe the course of action, the outcomes can be disastrous. Recall Robert McNamara's attempts to apply quantitative management to the Vietnam War, which led him to declare in May of 1962 that "every quantitative measurement we have shows that we're winning this war" (Sheehan 1988).

Thus real options analysis must remain more a process of reasoning that guides entrepreneurial decision-making and less an algorithm whose results command obedience. The exercise of good business judgment is why the best entrepreneurs and innovators get paid handsomely. Real options reasoning can provide a framework but not a substitute for this thought process. The same applies to scenario analysis, which offers a complementary approach to real options analysis, both as a means of discovering the most helpful options and as a way to estimate their value—and to this we now turn.

SCENARIO ANALYSIS: MANAGING RISK IN THE BUSINESS ENVIRONMENT

Scenario analysis can help innovators and entrepreneurs understand uncontrollable risk in the business environment and, armed with those insights, consider in advance what options should be developed and how these options should be valued.

Scenarios are stories, but of a very special kind. They portray logical, internally consistent futures that can be derived from current conditions in a rational manner— no interventions by flying saucer people allowed. The scenarios should set out dramatically different states of the business environment: for example, a scenario of stringent environmental constraints versus a scenario where emissions cost a company little; or, a world where concern with growth dominates national policies versus a world in which regulation and redistribution dominates. All scenarios must be relevant to some strategic decision before the company. And finally, there must be more than one—a single scenario effectively becomes a forecast.

We can illustrate the use of scenarios in evaluating a real option by returning to our EV Venture mini-case. The option before the company is to delay a major investment in manufacturing for one year anticipating some resolution of the uncertainties in the electric vehicle marketplace. This provides the strategic decision around which to build the analysis.

Next, we must define the principal risks. In addition to competitor risk, two external forces over which EV Venture has no control will determine the success of any electric vehicle launch. First, the effective price of competing liquid fuels, chiefly gasoline, provides the marketplace motivation for electric vehicles. Plainly a higher price provides greater incentives for consumers to purchase electric vehicles, while a low effective[3] price sends buyers back to their pick-up trucks.

Second, any new venture in the alternative vehicle space must be concerned with the consistency and durability of government support through regulation, consumer incentive, and research (National Research Council 2008). In the United States and around the globe, the EV market cannot be properly understood using normal business models because it is driven as much by government policies as by customers. The stability of these policies presents a difficult issue.

Having identified the chief sources of risk, we must now organize them to create meaningful scenarios. Practitioners have developed numerous methods to achieve this, and these will repay generously the time invested in their study (see Van der Heijden

UNITED STATES GOVERNMENT SUPPORT FOR ELECTRIC VEHICLES

Because the support programs of the federal government change unpredictably, both in magnitude and intent, any description of the government influence provides highly perishable information. The four distinct kinds of support on offer by late 2010 add strong supply and demand incentives to the more ordinary workings of the marketplace (U.S. Department of Energy 2010).

Purchaser Incentives. The federal government offered a $7,500 tax credit for purchasers of electric vehicles, and a proposal went before the Congress in early 2011 to convert this to a cash rebate available at the point of purchase.

Manufacturing Subsidies. The American Recovery and Reinvestment Act of 2009 provided:

- $2.4 billion in federal loans to three electric vehicle factories in Tennessee, Delaware, and California.
- $2 billion in grants to support 30 additional factories that produce batteries, motors, and other EV components. The recipients must match the federal contribution, but the effect is to reduce the private investment costs by 50 percent.

Government Purchases. In May of 2011 the General Services Administration (GSA) launched a pilot project to incorporate electric vehicles and technologies into the Federal fleet with an initial purchase of more than 100 electric vehicles. GSA will also establish the infrastructure for fueling and recharging at Federal buildings receiving the first round of vehicles (U.S. Department of Energy 2011).

Research and Development. The Department of Energy operates a Vehicle Technologies Program with a R&D budget of $165 million proposed for fiscal 2010 and focused heavily on electric powertrain vehicles.

Regulation. Recent increases in the Corporate Average Fuel Economy (CAFE) standards require vehicle manufacturers to increase fuel economy through 2016. Further increases beyond 2016 remain under consideration.

Notwithstanding the good intentions above, governments in all times and places have proven extraordinarily fickle—recall Cardinal Wolsey's famous "how wretched is that poor man that hangs on princes' favors."[4] Energy policy offers countless examples of unshakable political commitments that melted away in the heat of larger realities. This bipartisan malaise stretches from President Nixon's Project Independence, through President Carter's Synthetic Fuel Corporation, through President Clinton's Kyoto Agreement, to President Bush's promotion of a "hydrogen economy." Thus the prospect of policy instability requires EV Venture to comprehend the full implications of a business that "hangs on princes' favors."

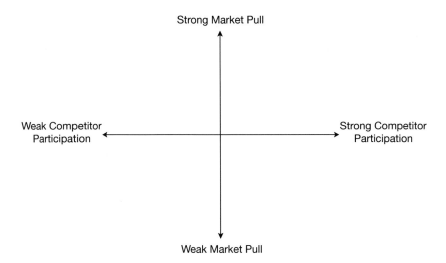

Figure 5.2. Market Risks for Electric Vehicles

2005, for example). For this exposition, we will use a graphical format, which often proves superior when communicating the analysis to a company's leadership or to investors. To represent the identified risks cleanly in two-dimensional space, we must consolidate them onto two axes.[5] The political uncertainty and fuel price uncertainty both operate in parallel, and so can be packaged together according to their effect— a strong electric vehicle market (high oil prices and continued government subsidies) or a weak, niche-like market (low oil prices and ineffectual government subsidies) as shown on the vertical axis of Figure 5.2. The horizontal axis measures competitor entry in the EV market, strong and immediate on the right and weak and delayed on the left.

The world of risk is now divided into four scenarios, and a story can be constructed for each to show the effect of that state of the world on the decision at issue.

Figure 5.3 summarizes these scenarios, but in reality they should be captured as substantive analytical documents, each containing "signposts," future events to watch for that suggest the world is or is not moving in that direction. In the case of EV Venture, these scenarios and signposts enable the company to test the issues raised by the real options analysis (Figure 5.1) against alternative narratives of the future.

For EV Venture and for any company, new or established, scenarios provide a virtual "wind tunnel" in which decision alternatives can be tested. The point is not to forecast which of these will take place, but rather to understand how each could influence the outcome of the decision. They allow the company to ask the essential question—*what would we do if this scenario actually did come to pass?*

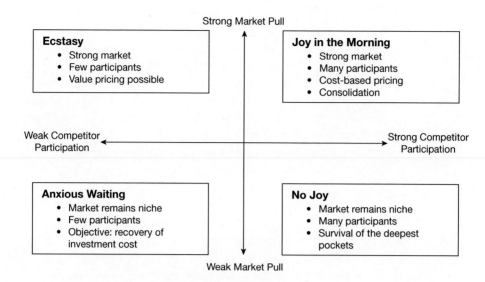

Figure 5.3. Market Scenarios for Electric Vehicles

BUILDING STRATEGY FROM SCENARIOS: THE CASE OF ARCH COAL

Success carries with it a unique set of risks: complacency, leading to panic when challenged by unpredicted events; over-reliance on an installed base of thinking, leading to myopia when confronting unanticipated opportunities and threats; and a failure to challenge precedents that had served so well to date.

Consider IBM, which had ridden its 1982 introduction of the personal computer to such prosperity that its stock price had tripled by 1987. But this success masked the seeds of later trouble. Profits began to erode under severe competition from PC clones using MS DOS and Intel chips and from IBM's failure to introduce its own operating system in competition with Microsoft. At the same time, the traditional mainframe business declined under pressure from low-cost, smaller scale computing. Caught without strategic alternatives, IBM saw its stock price plunge from a 1987 high of nearly $45 per share to $10 per share by 1994. In 1993, a new management team led by Louis Gerstner had to be brought in to resurrect a company that many analysts left for dead.

IBM did indeed make a comeback, and the company moved beyond the mainframe and PC to build a business around services and software. By early 2011 its market capitalization had surpassed that of Google. But much of the pain that the company, its workers, and its shareholders experienced in achieving that happy condition might have been avoided had the company not let its success mask the need for change. A series of interviews with IBM executives, conducted in 1990 by Professor David Yoffie of the Harvard Business School, had revealed the need to develop strategic alternatives. But action was not taken until the company was in crisis. As Professor Yoffie later observed, "It's really hard to move a company when it's doing well and not facing a crisis" (Lohr 2011).

Arch Coal was facing a similar dilemma by the end of 2005. Arch, a St. Louis coal company operating low-sulfur mines in Appalachia and the western states, was noted within the industry for its high-productivity mines and culture of safe operations. Excellence in operations, however, is never sufficient in a commodity business. In addition, exogenous political and market forces must mesh favorably with well-run operations. And in the 2000–5 period, they were doing just that. CEO Steven F. Leer noted this strong tail wind in a 2005 investor conference (Leer 2005):

- the price of natural gas, a principal competing fossil fuel, had risen sharply relative to coal, and most forecasts indicated this would remain a condition of the market;
- electric utilities, Arch's principal customers, had recently announced 65,000 mW of new coal-fired power plants; and
- low-sulfur coal was gaining a compelling advantage in the marketplace, while Arch enjoyed a strong reserve base of this coal.

Reflecting market success, the stock price had risen by a factor of four from early 2003 to the end of 2005. As a result, Arch entered 2006 with a strong balance sheet and investor expectations for future earnings. However, the company's leadership recognized the transient nature of such favorable conditions, and so began a strategic planning process seeking ways to mitigate the inevitable reversal of fortune. The process that Arch followed illustrates the key principles underlying the use of scenarios to mitigate a major strategic risk.

USING SCENARIOS TO BUILD STRATEGY

Consider the dynamics of the Arch Coal decision process as it began in 2005–6. On the one hand, the success of the previous years provided little apparent motivation to consider changing anything about the business model or the company strategy. But those experienced in commodity markets understood that the favorable conditions that had buoyed success could depart as unexpectedly as they had come. And if strategic alternatives were to be explored, far better to do it from a position of strength—a good balance sheet and high stock price. At the same time, however, any capital investment would be measured in billions of dollars, and would have to earn durable returns in a volatile market and regulatory environment far into an unforeseeable future—essentially the business conditions described at the beginning of this chapter.

The strategy development process employed by Arch illustrates the fundamental principles that reside at the heart of successful scenario planning.

Principle 1: Top Management Involvement

The value of strategic planning with scenarios comes from the thought process and not from any written document. To be sure, written documentation of each step in the process helps provide a stable point of departure for the inevitable mid-course corrections. But this document must be created and owned by the company's strategic leadership. Consultants can facilitate, as was the case with Arch,[6] but the thinking behind the scenarios and the strategic options must be that of the company's leadership. Otherwise no change can happen. In the Arch Coal process, CEO Steven Leer led the management team that developed and used the scenarios. This leadership team remained engaged throughout the process.

Principle 2: Ask the Right Question

To be useful in strategy development, the scenarios should be built around a question that is broad enough to include the principal options, but focused enough to properly test the consequences of each. When the company is in crisis, the circumstances of the crisis make this relatively straightforward. But when it is not, when a benign business environment complements the operating strengths of the company, the choice of focal question presents a greater challenge. Such was the case with Arch. Continued growth was at the heart of the company's strategic intent, and so the leadership team chose for its focal question "How do we optimize our growth opportunities in a changing world?"

Principle 3: Include the Chief Uncertainties Influencing the Outcome

Asking the right question directs the strategic conversation toward the external uncertainties that will exert the most influence on the outcome of each strategic option. To capture these uncertainties, the Arch team constructed the kind of graphic representation discussed earlier—reproduced as Figure 5.4.

The horizontal axis captures the strong connectivity between energy use and economic growth.[7] To the right resides a world of strong growth and hence strong primary energy demand—to the left, the opposite. And the vertical axis captures the place of coal within that growth. At the top of the vertical axis, coal and coal-derived fuels find regulatory and market favor. A variety of external conditions could lead to that world, especially: mitigation of the chief climate change consequences from the use of coal, perhaps through unanticipated technologies that enable low-cost carbon capture and sequestration; high costs for competing fuels, especially natural gas; and limitations on nuclear, wind, and photovoltaic alternatives. In contrast, the bottom of the vertical axis portrays an opposite world in which environmental concerns and/or competition effectively prevent the expansion of coal.

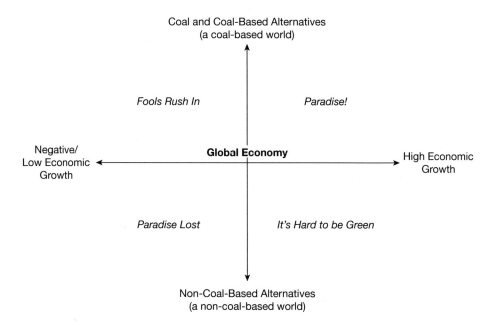

Figure 5.4. Arch Coal Scenario Framework

Principle 4: Test Each Strategic Option in Each Scenario to Ascertain Consequences

The scenario in each quadrant should be described in sufficient detail that the full implications for the current business model and for each strategic option can be discerned. Each scenario should be given a label that captures its essence well. These labels become a shorthand for the strategy team's ongoing conversations. The Arch labels appear in Figure 5.4. Then the performance of each strategic option can be compared with the base case of current strategy on a consistent basis.

Principle 5: Include Wild Card Scenarios

Users of scenarios should not assume that all uncertainties can be captured in a fourfold worldview—the future is too messy a place for that. In addition, special conditions should also be considered: the "wild card" scenario. One example might be escalating political instability in the Middle East, perhaps culminating in a Sunni–Shiite war. This would almost certainly lead to protracted physical disruptions in oil supplies with extreme consequences for oil-consuming economies around the world. Arch Coal employed similarly specialized scenarios to explore options for converting coal to liquid fuels or to synthetic gas.

Principle 6: Learning the Art of Strategic Conversation

Using scenarios as a framework for strategic reasoning should not be a one-off event. Instead, the process should enable an ongoing strategic conversation among the leadership team, continually testing the strategic choices made against the always-evolving, inevitably surprising state of the world. In effect, the scenarios hold up a strategic lens through which Arch or any company can view past decisions and learn from their outcomes. CEO Leer keeps a copy of the basic scenario document on his desk, using it as a point of departure from which to consider unfolding events.

EPILOGUE: THE POWER OF PESSIMISTIC THINKING

From the perspective of mid-2011, CEO Steven Leer reflected on the value that Arch Coal had gained from its investment in scenario planning. He noted that the project had not been inexpensive—chiefly, occupying the time and attention of the most talented leaders in the company for about 18 months. But in exchange, Arch gained the power of strategic paranoia.[8]

As the management team began to construct their scenarios, they noted that historically shareholder value had varied with (a) the performance of the U.S. economy and (b) the regulatory/political environment for coal. These became the horizontal and vertical axes for the scenario matrix of Figure 5.4. In the years immediately following the scenario process, the more benign business conditions continued, and a prospering economy generally overcame a softening coal market. Despite this, the Arch team focused their attention (and their paranoia) on the negative futures of the scenario mix, especially the southwest quadrant.

That pessimistic focus led to several strategic insights. First, the policy uncertainty surrounding "thermal" coal, which is burned in electric power plants and accounts for the majority of tons shipped, would probably not apply in equal measure to metallurgical coal, which is used in steel making.[9] Second, the emerging growth economies, especially in Asia, would offer attractive markets for metallurgical coal, which was attractive for export because of its high price per ton. This suggested an exporting strategy. Third, a detailed analysis showed that most coal companies had overestimated the amount of high-quality reserves they held and took the estimates of the others at face value. Hence, the market seemed headed toward a period of supply constraints. This suggested that a strong position in metallurgical coal would offer high returns even in a delayed economic recovery. And finally, the likelihood of continued tightening of regulatory requirements for safety and the environment would militate in favor of the operators who already did this well.

The strategy that emerged from these insights included the acquisition of a major supplier of metallurgical coal, International Coal Group, in the spring of 2011 and a continuing investment in safety and environmental protection. To be sure, none of this insulated Arch from the sharp economic recession that began in 2008, and the price per share fell from a high of $72.79 in June of 2008 to a low of $12.59 by December of that year. But even in a delayed recovery, the strategy derived from scenario thinking has enabled a positive response and a better outcome than would otherwise have been possible.

IN CONCLUSION

The value of real options reasoning and scenario analysis does not derive from their ability to reveal unambiguous conclusions as a substitute for human judgment. Employed properly, these tools can empower strategic judgment with framework and institutional memory, and they can communicate that judgment throughout the strategic leadership team.

NOTES

1. Real options offer less help with execution risk, the possibility that the innovating company or entrepreneur is simply not capable of implementing the project.
2. These business models enable subscribers to reserve and rent a light duty vehicle, chiefly for use in and around urban areas. See: www.zipcar.com, or www.car2go.com.
3. We should understand "effective price" to mean the combination of: (a) the underlying fuel price, historically highly volatile and depending heavily upon the political stability of the oil-producing nations; and (b) the ability of increasingly efficient internal combustion powertrains to convert fuel into mobility services.
4. William Shakespeare, *Henry VIII*, Act III, Scene 2.
5. Good practice also encourages development of "wild card" scenarios, plausible chains of events that cannot be captured well on two axes. Their use helps avoid the trap of excessive neatness in an inherently untidy world.
6. For the Arch strategy development, a facilitation team was engaged: Palomar Consulting, led by Dr. F. Lee Van Horn. The chapter author participated as a member of this team.
7. To be sure, primary energy use per dollar of GDP continues to fall, especially in the OECD nations. Nevertheless, most projections of future energy use depend heavily on world economic growth.
8. As Intel CEO Andrew Grove noted in his book with the same title, "Only the paranoid survive."
9. Metallurgical coal (also called coking coal) is first converted to coke through heating the coal in an oxygen-free environment. After the coke is produced, it is added to iron ore in another high-temperature environment to produce iron. Every ton of steel made in a traditional blast furnace requires 0.6 tons of metallurgical coal. In general, coking coal is valued at almost twice the price of thermal coal.

REFERENCES

Adner, R. and Levinthal, D. (2004) "What is *Not* a Real Option: Considering Boundaries for the Application of Real Options to Business Strategy," *Academy of Management Review*, 29 (1): 74–85.

Amram, M. and Kulatilaka, N. (1999) *Real Options: Managing Strategic Investment in an Uncertain World*. Boston: Harvard Business School Press.

Bowman, E. H. and Hurry, D. (1993) "Strategy Through the Option Lens: An Integrated View of Resource Investments and the Incremental-Choice Process," *Academy of Management Review*, 18: 760–782.

Ernst & Young (September 2010) *Cleantech Matters: The Electrification of Transportation: Vision to Reality*. Available at: http://www.ey.com/GL/en/Services/Strategic-Growth-Markets/Cleantech-matters---The-electrification-of-transportation--from-vision-to-reality.

Ferreira, N., Kar, J., and Trigeorgis, Lenos (2009) "Option Games: The Key to Competing in Capital Intensive Industries," *Harvard Business Review*, March: 101–107.

Grenadier, Steven (Ed.) (2000) *Game Choices: The Intersection of Real Options and Game Theory*. London: Risk Publications.

Leer, Steven F. (2005) Presentation at the Howard Weil 33rd Annual Energy Conference, New Orleans. April 6.

Lohr, Steve (2011) "Lessons in Longevity from IBM," *New York Times*, April 18.

McGrath, R. G., Ferrier, W., and Mendelow, A. (2004) "Real Options as Engines of Choice and Heterogeneity," *Academy of Management Review*, 29 (1): 86–101.

National Research Council: Committee on Assessment of Resource Needs for Fuel Cell and Hydrogen Technologies (2008) *Transitions to Alternative Transportation Technologies – A Focus on Hydrogen*. Washington, DC: National Academies Press.

Rogers, J. (2009) *Strategy, Value, and Risk: The Real Options Approach*. New York: Palgrave Macmillan.

Sheehan, Neil (1988) *A Bright Shining Lie*. New York: Random House.

Trigeorgis, Lenos (2000) *Real Options: Managerial Flexibility and Strategy in Resource Allocation*. Cambridge, MA: MIT Press.

U.S. Department of Energy (February 2010) *One Million Electric Vehicles By 2015*.

U.S. Department of Energy (2011) Press release, May 24. Available at: www.energy.gov/news/10344.htm.

Van der Heijden, K. (2005) *Scenarios: The Art of Strategic Conversation*. New York: John Wiley and Sons.

PART III

Open Innovation: New Horizons, New Risks

The places I hiked to!
The roads that I rambled
To find the best eggs
That have ever been scrambled!
If you want to get eggs
you can't buy at the store,
you have to do things
never thought of before.

Scrambled Eggs Super! Dr. Seuss

WHETHER A CORPORATE INNOVATOR or an independent entrepreneur, you should bear in mind that nearly the entire population of the universe is made up of others. Those others have ideas. Some of their ideas are good, some are not so good, and some are outright dangerous. But if you can sort out which are which, and then figure out how to mesh the best with your own enterprise, you will enjoy a distinct advantage over your competitors: an innovation cycle that offers a wider scope of opportunity, reduces cycle time from invention to marketplace, and costs less. This section of *Chance and Intent* can help you understand how to do that.

THE CHANGING FACE OF INNOVATION

In the United States and around the world, the process of innovation is being reshaped by five persistent and fundamental forces: (a) the spread of science and engineering capabilities around the world, which increases the number of competitors and their quality; (b) the rise of innovation and entrepreneurship around the world as a pathway to economic growth; (c) the convergence of technology sectors previously thought distinct, which allows opportunities and dangers to arise from unfamiliar areas; (d) systemic shifts in industry architecture, which change the basis for innovation; and (e) a new, intense global competition characterized by more rapid product cycles from invention to commodity.

The Global Dispersion of Capabilities in Science and Engineering

In the years following World War II, the OECD nations enjoyed a near-monopoly on science and engineering, the basic stuff from which technology-based innovation springs. But more recently, these capabilities have dispersed and become highly competitive around the world. China, for example, increased its research and development investment as a fraction of GDP at an annual rate of 5.7 percent from 2001 to 2007. In contrast, U.S. R&D investment relative to GDP fell at an annual rate of 0.5 percent over the same period (U.S. National Academy of Sciences 2010).

The availability of skilled people is also diffusing. Currently China graduates more English-speaking engineers than the United States graduates engineers. Quality has also improved. Many consider China's Tsinghua University, Peking University, and Shanghai Jiao Tong University among the world's foremost academic institutions. Elsewhere, the Indian Institute of Technology joins that elite group (U.S. National Academy of Sciences 2010).

The Rise of Innovation and Entrepreneurship

Innovation and entrepreneurship have flourished around the world in response to the economic liberalization of many formerly managed economies, especially in Asia. A sample of 59 countries that include about half the world's population and 84 percent of global GDP suggests that about 110 million people were actively engaged in starting a business and an additional 140 million were running a business formed in the past three-and-a-half years (Kelly et al. 2010). While many of these could not be considered technology-based, those that are provide intense competition. Consider Chinese entrepreneur John Deng, CEO of the chipmaker Vimicro. His company holds some 400 patents and is the world's leading supplier of PC camera processor chips. "We have moved from 'manufactured in China' to 'designed in China,'" Deng observed (Silverthorne 2005).

Value-Creation through Convergence

Scientific and engineering advances in seminal fields like microelectronics or genetics can offer unexpected opportunities (and risks) at the interface with traditional business models. For example, the well-known convergence of the traditional telephone and the microprocessor led to a variety of powerful, convenient, and portable devices that offer new models of service and opportunities for new business providers.

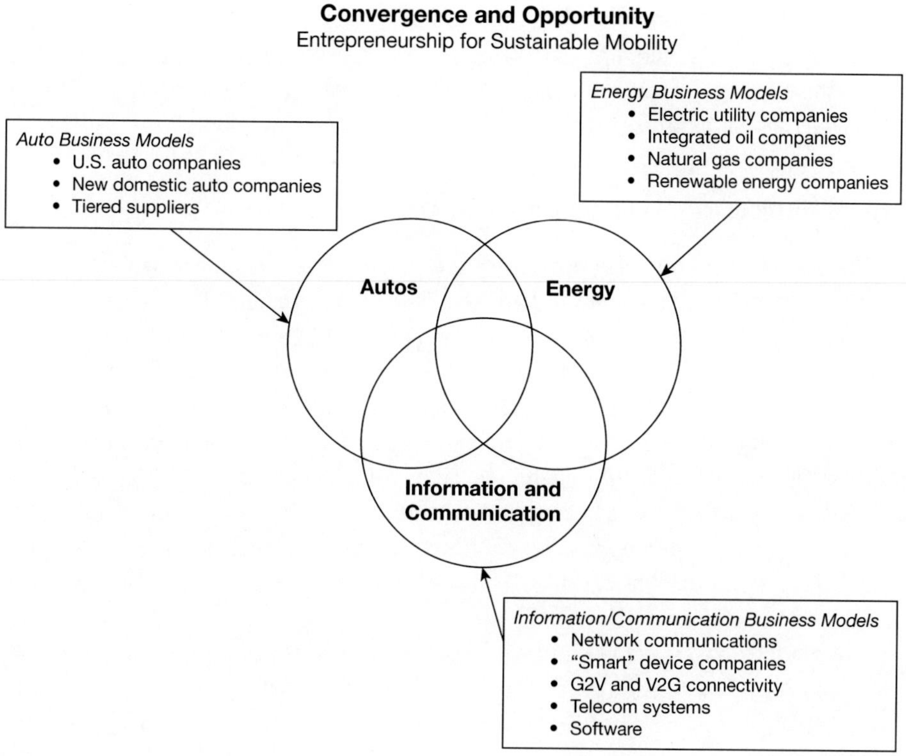

Convergence and Opportunity
Entrepreneurship for Sustainable Mobility

Figure III.1 Convergence and Opportunity: Entrepreneurship for Sustainable Mobility

We can now see this convergence appearing in sectors once thought to be the domain of traditional business models—road mobility, for example. Auto companies, information/communication companies, and energy companies find their once-distinct business models converging, especially around the electric powertrain vehicle.[1] The common product, the electric powertrain automobile, is evolving toward a traveling platform to which safety, refueling, and information services all add value to the basic mobility service, as shown in Figure III.1.

Consider refueling, for example. Consumers could realize more value from their plug-in hybrid or all-electric vehicles if they had the opportunity to recharge at any place and time, thus extending the electric range of these vehicles independent of the pace of battery improvements. This requires the widespread availability of local electric infrastructures to provide the necessary charging stations, which brings into the value chain the electric utilities. In addition, a standard means of billing for the electricity used must be adopted. And finally, real-time information about traffic conditions and the availability of charging stations can allow efficient energy management. Yet other infrastructures can provide the source of this information by allowing connectivity between the vehicle and the roadway, the vehicle and other vehicles, or the vehicle and satellite networks. In isolation, the traditional business models of auto companies, energy companies, and other infrastructure providers like information/ communication companies cannot take full advantage of the opportunities at the intersection of these domains. But within the converging domains of Figure III.1 reside the best new opportunities to create customer value. The car is no longer exclusively an auto company thing.

Trends in Industry Architecture

We use the term "industry architecture" to mean the arrangement of firms across the value chain. In a completely vertically integrated architecture, the competing firms would control (perhaps own) all the value-added steps from product development through final sales. Consider, for example, a vertically integrated oil company like Exxon, which owns all the steps in the value chain from exploration through production and refining to the retail outlets that sell motor fuels. In a completely horizontal industry architecture, each step in the chain of value-added activities would be controlled by a distinct set of firms. The personal computer industry today offers the best example, and most of the industry has adopted variants of the Dell business model. Pure cases are hard to find, but most industries tend toward the one or the other.

Technology-based industries tend to start with a largely vertical architecture, which enables a firm to capture fully the rewards of a successful campaign of research, development, and innovation. But if the industry architecture begins to shift toward a more horizontal model, then value capture is at risk for companies that retain the vertical model, and alternative business processes for innovation become necessary. Consider the computer industry, for example. By the 1950s, the principal computer manufacturers were established firms in the office equipment or consumer electronics business: IBM, RCA, Sperry Rand, and the like. These competitors occupied the most essential steps in the value chain: software (including applications) and the machine itself. In those days, the machine and its software functioned as an integrated whole. Software design was tied closely to the hardware configuration of a particular machine and not usable outside that machine. But with the emergence of a dominant design, the IBM 360, this linkage began to weaken. The spectacular commercial success of the IBM 360 created a generic platform for developing programs that could be run on a large installed base, and common programs and programming techniques began to emerge (Mowery and Rosenberg 1998).

The introduction of the personal computer by IBM in 1981 accelerated the industry shift toward a more horizontal architecture. This shift came from three consequential decisions: (a) to outsource the operating system to a new company called Microsoft; (b) to outsource the processor to a company called Intel; and (c) to provide an open platform for application writers to create programs attractive to users. To be sure, these decisions were taken more from competitive necessity than from strategic calculation. But they did allow IBM to create the dominant design of the personal computer—simply labeled the IBM PC.

At its introduction, IBM PC was neither the first nor the best on the market—those distinctions would fall to Apple. But it was the first to combine enough features that were in demand by business users with the IBM cachet, which lowered the acquisition risk perceived by corporate purchasing departments. And so the IBM PC quickly gained the market leader position with its open-architecture platform (Bodde 2004).

Soon specialized firms originating outside the PC industry began to produce superior memory and other chips. Specialized industries for disk drives, monitors, screens, and other peripherals also developed. Yet another distinct industry wrote software, especially for applications, which is what users want anyway. Some companies (notably Dell) even focused on distribution infrastructure. And so the once vertical industry architecture quickly delaminated into a more horizontal architecture in which particular firms specialized in the newly created layers. The entire basis for competition changed, and IBM is no longer in the business.

An engaging bit of history, to be sure, but also one that is likely to play again in other sectors. An accumulation of evidence shows a strong connection between the architecture of a product like the computer and the architecture of the industry that brings it to market. In computers, the growing modularity of the machine enabled the rapid shift in architecture for the PC industry (Pisano and Teece 2007).

In other sectors, however, inherent characteristics of the product itself have made modularization difficult. An automobile must perform as a coherent unit at high speed and sometimes under inept operation. And because the product architecture is integral, complex interactions can occur among the thousands of components. In contrast the performance of your computer screen or printer does not affect the performance of the computer. And while screens or printers are interchangeable among manufacturers, this is not the case with most auto parts. Nevertheless, recent years have seen vehicles trending toward a more modular architecture, a response to the need for faster, less costly innovation and manufacturing (Moavenzadeh 2006). Batteries, the key component of electric vehicles, are rapidly becoming interchangeable. If this trend persists, history suggests that the architecture of the auto industry is likely to change in response, and with that change, new models for innovation will surely arise.

The New Competition

All the foregoing have contributed to more rapid product innovation cycles, which leave the innovator with less time to recover the costs of developing the new products and services. For example, an analysis of 39 distinct technology generations across 12 product markets showed a marked reduction in the time from innovation to marketplace takeoff (Stremersch et al. 2009). And when an end-of-cycle technology becomes a commodity, fierce price competition replaces early-market innovation as the basis of competition. This new competition requires faster development cycles, less costly development cycles, and an ability to reach profitability at lower manufacturing volumes than in the past.

TOWARD MORE OPEN INNOVATION MODELS

These five forces augur ill for the models of research, development, and innovation that have served so well in the years through World War II and the immediate postwar period. The history of the microelectronics revolution, as captured by Mowery and Rosenberg, illustrates this well.

> In a virtual reversal of the prewar situation, the R&D facilities of large firms provided many of the basic technological advances that new, smaller firms commercialized. Small entrants' role in the introduction of new products, reflected in their often-dominant share of markets in new semiconductor devices, significantly outstripped that of larger firms. Moreover, the role of new firms grew in importance with the development of the integrated circuit.
>
> (Mowery and Rosenberg 1998: 132)

As a consequence of these five persistent trends, processes of innovation around the globe are becoming more dispersed and pluralistic. The heart of the matter is not whether large firms are superior to entrepreneurial startups—or whether the reverse is true. Rather the core issue for the contemporary innovator and entrepreneur is how these can be combined for the greater good. This requires skills in more open models of innovation, and that is what Part III of *Chance and Intent* is all about.

NEW HORIZONS, NEW RISKS

We begin with Chapter 6, "Open Innovation from Theory to Practice," by John T. Wilbanks, former Vice President of Creative Commons, a non-profit organization seeking to achieve an open content Internet. Wilbanks' chapter speaks to the early difficulties encountered as inexperienced companies sought to adopt a more open framework. The chapter notes the many unresolved issues that remain as open innovation concepts migrate from their software origins to a wider field of application. Then follows Chapter 7, "The Uses and Risks of Open Innovation," by James A. Euchner, a principal at Princeton Growth Partners and Visiting Scientist at the MIT Sloan School of Management. Euchner addresses the strategic implications of two forms of open innovation: *open boundary innovation*, which modifies but generally preserves the business model of the firms adopting it, and *open source innovation*, which tends to disrupt the established business model. He offers practical advice for innovators and strategists considering either approach. And finally, Robert Laubacher, a research scientist at MIT's Center for Collective Intelligence, offers Chapter 8, "Entrepreneurship and Venture Capital in the Age of Collective Intelligence." Laubacher views web-enabled collective intelligence as a "genome," which finds unique expression in different business models. He argues that collective intelligence might exert as profound influence on innovation in the twenty-first century as the emergence of the venture capital industry and the venture-backed startup did in the latter half of the twentieth century.

To be sure, much remains to be invented, especially innovation markets and business models that could carry open innovation beyond the narrow domain of information products, where it has thus far flourished. However, promising experiments are being conducted. In September of 2010, for example, Clemson University and the American Society of Mechanical Engineers (ASME)[2] demonstrated the anchor service for an open innovation network designed to accelerate the pace of innovation in the auto industry. This demonstration, called the *AutoVenture Forum* (AVF), marks the first time that an open innovation service has been attempted at the industry level. The purpose of AVF is to link selected entrepreneurial companies with the technology base, systems integration, manufacturing, and market channels of the established auto industry. Four important lessons for managing open innovation at the industry level emerged from this project: (a) the tiered supply industry forms the essential link between the OEM and the entrepreneurs because it solves the scale-up issue; (b) supply chain innovation builds job creation; (c) a high-quality flow of deal-ready entrepreneurs is essential to attract industry participation; and (d) industry leadership will be required to establish the complete innovation network (Bodde et al. 2011).

Much remains to be done if open innovation processes are to serve as the dominant industrial paradigm—as the football coaches' cliché has it, "Their future is still ahead of them." But where they work, they can profoundly change the opportunities and risks for corporate innovators and entrepreneurs alike.

NOTES

1.   Within the term "electric powertrain vehicle" we include hybrid electric vehicles, plug-in hybrid electric vehicles, hydrogen fuel cell vehicles, and all-electric vehicles. Each of these can be considered a mobile infrastructure of electronic systems that provide motive power, information, navigation, entertainment, and similar services.
2.   This project was supported by a grant from the U.S. Department of Energy, by *Breakthrough Innovation* funds from ASME, and by Clemson University.

REFERENCES

Bodde, David L. (2004) *The Intentional Entrepreneur.* Armonk: M. E. Sharpe.
Bodde, D. L., Skardon, John N., and Byler, Ethan (2011) "The AutoVenture Forum: Demonstrating a New Process for Managing Automotive Innovation," *IEEE International Technology Management Conference 2011,* San Jose, p. 964.
Kelly, Donna J., Bosma, Neils, and Amoros, Jose Ernesto (2010) "Global Entrepreneurship Monitor." Babson College, Boston and Universidad del Desarrollo, Chile. Available at: www.gemconsortium.org.
Moavenzadeh, John (2006) "Offshoring Automotive Engineering: Globalization and Footprint Strategy in the Motor Vehicle Industry." National Academy of Engineering, Washington, DC.
Mowery, David C. and Rosenberg, Nathan (1998) *Paths of Innovation.* New York: Cambridge University Press.
Pisano, Gary P. and Teece, David J. (2007) "How to Capture Value from Innovation: Shaping Intellectual Property and Industry Architecture," *California Management Review,* 50 (1): 278–296.

Silverthorne, Sean (2005) "The Rise of Innovation in Asia," in *Working Knowledge*, March 7. Boston: Harvard Business School. Available at: http://hbswk.hbs.edu/item/4676.html.

Stremersch, S., Muller, Eitan, and Peres, Renana (2009) "Does New Product Growth Accelerate across Technology Generations?" Published with open access at Springerlink.com.

U.S. National Academy of Sciences (2010) *Rising Above the Gathering Storm Revisited: Rapidly Approaching Category 5*. Washington, DC: National Academies Press.

Chapter 6

Open Innovation from Theory to Practice

JOHN T. WILBANKS

MANY OLDER THEORIES OF INNOVATION hold that success in breakthrough research and development springs from control by the innovating firm: control of ideas, of knowledge, of data, and most importantly of the intellectual property rights that governed the copying and use of the ideas, knowledge, and data. For most of the twentieth century, this control-based approach worked. Large, centralized laboratories sprang up out of government research via the National Laboratories system in the United States, and out of massively successful technology companies like Bell, General Electric, and Xerox.

However, many of the most important inventions that originated in Bell Laboratories or the Xerox Palo Alto Research Center (PARC) were completely missed as innovations by laboratory management. It was not until those innovations spun out into new places and new companies, funded by private venture capital and staffed by a new class of mobile knowledge workers, that the computer mouse and the concept of windows-driven computer "desktops" made the leap from concept to reality. The advent of mobile workers and private capital has been augmented by personal computing and digital networks, creating a remarkable cycle of innovation in technology and culture.

We now stand at a point when the small firm and the individual are capable of playing much larger roles in innovation cycles alongside massive companies than ever possible inside an industrialized culture.

Enormous amounts of know-how have been embedded into widely available tools, from computer-aided design for architectural work (like Google *Sketch Up*) to object-oriented software packages (like the wildly popular *Ruby on Rails* programming environment). As a result, individuals can independently design and manufacture innovations for consumer goods, technologies, and even genetically modified bacteria. The innovation system itself is being subjected to radical innovation, although the funders and institutions involved in the traditional research and development culture are not only slow to catch onto the change, but in some cases, actively serve as drags on the newer forms of innovation.

This chapter briefly explores the theory of open innovation (OI), and then moves on to the infrastructure needed to make the theory useful to business practitioners. The chapter closes with a brief section on the need for appropriate business models to exploit the new innovation ecosystems. Although open innovation remains a relatively novel business process, those wishing to implement it in their business can significantly increase their odds of success by paying close attention to existing standards efforts, leveraging existing infrastructure, and focusing on the creation of locally appropriate models to capture the value created in the OI process, most of which fall outside traditional business models.

OPEN INNOVATION: FOUNDATIONS

Open innovation is closely associated with Henry Chesbrough, a professor at the University of California Haas School of Business. Open innovation explores the potential of any institution—firms, universities, research institutions—to take advantage of the efficiencies possible in a networked environment.

Most of the smart people, as Joy's Law notes, have always worked somewhere else. But a network culture offers the opportunity to connect more and more of those smart people to an institution's mission: to contribute to internal projects from the outside; to take a project that fails to gather internal support forward using outside funding; to generate novel projects outside and "spin into" new internal projects. All of this becomes possible as the transaction costs required to move the knowledge fall. These are the efficiencies promised by the theory of open innovation.

Open innovation depends on the fundamental "leakage" of knowledge from inside the firm to the external world. This comes from many sources depending on the kind of institution performing the R&D. It could be publication via scholarly journal, by patent, by conference presentation, or more currently via blog post or wiki edit. It could be via conversation at a networking event or social occasion. It could be accidental, as when a 4th Generation iPhone was left in a San Jose bar, to be dismantled and documented by bloggers. Knowledge is tough to contain.

The core insight for the practice of open innovation is that business must intentionally invert the concept of leakage. Knowledge must flow in and out of an institution as a purposeful thing, not an accidental process. Thus managed knowledge leakage becomes central to the operation of open innovation processes and not a flaw in the process—a feature, not a bug, as the programmers say. OI manages the movement of knowledge, letting a firm use the world outside an institution to generate internally useful knowledge. Thus the core skill for success in open innovation is the management of information and knowledge flows across company boundaries.

The last important element of open innovation theory is the business model. A world of purposeful information flow conflicts with many of the business structures of the last 50 years—especially intellectual property rights. Copyrights govern the copying, distribution, and reuse of the documents containing actionable knowledge, from software to scholarship. Trade secrets and knowledge leakage on the public web oppose one another fundamentally. And patents inhibit institutions from acting on useful knowledge, even if the action would be far afield from the business concerns of the patent owner.

EMERGING RULES OF THE ROAD

To date, the standardization of the network has been largely technocratic. That standardization enables an open innovation paradigm to emerge as a possibility, but does not yet enable the horizontal spread of open innovation, because each company must develop its own strategy for assembling the set of technologies needed for each opportunity together with the package of rights needed to use those technologies. There is not yet the standard legal framework to allow recombination of technologies with freedom to go to market, nor the semantic standardization to allow for easy discovery of relevant technologies via a search engine or online marketplace, required to realize the full potential of the open innovation theory.

Legal standardization is a relatively new concept, one that emerges from the experience of free/libre open source software and free culture. Open source software as we know it today emerged as a reaction to the increasing application of control via copyright licenses over software, and most open source software adheres to a tradeoff made between software creators and those who wish to reuse and remake that software: the owner grants the right to make copies and make changes, but the recipient has to play by certain rules for those rights to exist.

These rules can include attribution—the right to be given credit for one's work—and "copyleft"—when changes are made and distributed, those changes in turn have to be made available under the same terms. But these simple ideas turn out to be complex to implement, and a cascade of software copyright licenses is often created. And it turns out that the actual drafting of the licenses can affect the ability to recombine and reuse two pieces of "free" software if the legal terms are not precisely standardized. The problem is known as license proliferation, and results in the legal incompatibility of open tools.

In free culture (creative copyrighted works) this problem has been largely averted by the advent of the Creative Commons suite of copyright licenses, which cover a spectrum of rights and obligations in a standardized form. Even within the Creative Commons suite, there are some fundamental differences of opinion that impinge on interoperability. For example, the option to prevent a derivative work from being made is incompatible with the option of copyleft. However, the overall impact of a single suite of standards in the cultural licensing space has allowed an explosion of cultural works into the global digital commons that provides a good lesson for open innovation overall. There is remarkable power in the implementation of legal "openness" via a small set of choices, a limited spectrum of obligations, and a fundamental, pre-negotiated "right to use" at the core (in this case, to make copies), all supported by an organization committed to long-term stewardship of the legal standards. This allows both individuals and the corporations to adopt systems for their own purposes, but via standardization, creates the chance for their knowledge to flow between themselves without the friction of negotiation.

SOME IMPORTANT DISTINCTIONS

Open innovation is often conflated with two other theories of modern innovation— "user-driven innovation" (UDI), and "distributed innovation" (DI). It's worth the time to understand these theories and how they differ from OI.

UDI focuses on the individual innovator, who tends to be an end user with an idea to improve a product. In UDI, the innovation comes from being "close" to the problem, or alternately we say the knowledge required to innovate is "sticky" and doesn't move far from the user. The core insight is that if the end user of a product has the power to change and improve the product, she is very likely to do so, irrespective of intellectual property rights. The user in the classic UDI system cares more about functionality than about IP protection, and thus, the essential components of UDI are democratic access to the systems necessary for innovation in the user's context: the toolbox, the prototyping facility, the ability to test.

Distributed innovation builds on a truly disruptive aspect of the network, which is the innovation power of a collected set of individuals whose individual actions "snap together" into a coherent group through standard technical systems and digital networks. This is a completely novel ecosystem for innovation, and two good examples are the online encyclopedia Wikipedia and the open source software development culture and methodology. In each case, problems are solved without a central authority assigning tasks and without the maximalist approach to intellectual property associated with traditional forms of innovation diffusion and exploitation. Rather, the communities are formed by many different individuals, participating for very different sets of reasons and incentives, who self-organize around challenges and tasks. As such, the "designed DI" system has proven quite difficult to achieve. However, the power of distributed innovation can be seen in many of the "semi-closed" web 2.0 platforms such as the iPhone application store, Facebook, Twitter, and more, which each use an ecosystem approach to engage users in a distributed but closed innovation environment.

It is vital for practitioners to choose whether they seek to engage in open, user-driven, or distributed innovation. Each one carries a different set of requirements and infrastructure, and each one implies a different business model.

User-driven is perhaps the easiest: it is most relevant to firms in the acquisition sense. A company that stays close to its users is most likely to benefit, by acquiring a user-generated innovation, improving its design and packaging, and then marketing it. The primary change is not therefore in the business model, but in the customer relationship, and the infrastructure is simply whether or not the user has the tools needed to make a breakthrough. Distributed innovation is much harder to create from scratch. DI requires an entire ecosystem to flourish: the expertise and ability required to contribute must be widely distributed, and easily gained. Business models that revolve around services and communities appear to be the key to building successful firms around DI, with good examples in technology like Red Hat (selling services around the Linux operating system) and outside technology like Threadless (selling low-quantity, high-quality, community-designed-and-selected T-shirts).

Open innovation sits in a very different ecosystem from either UDI or DI, however. The decision to move toward an open innovation approach is entirely within the control of the firm, and does not depend nearly as much on the efforts of individuals as either UDI or DI. The key elements of OI in some cases cut across traditional business practices in ways that can create friction inside the firm, and those elements also often exist without the sorts of essential support structures that underpin traditional approaches to managing and exploiting innovation-related knowledge. Open innovation depends on changes in the very behavior of firms and its implementation depends on the successful satisfaction of a new requirements set.

CONDITIONS FOR THE PRACTICE OF OPEN INNOVATION

Chesbrough's theory of OI is a good starting point for practitioners to understand the requirements, as he lays out three key conditions for OI to succeed as a practical business strategy. First, there must be a *purposeful* inflow and outflow of institutional or firm knowledge. Second, there must be an external market with the capacity to support innovation. And third, the firm must have a revenue model that allows for the monetization of the value created by open innovation.

First Condition: Opening the Gates of Knowledge Flow

The purposeful inflow and outflow of knowledge, Chesbrough's first condition, presents the practitioner with requirements related to information, incentives, institutions, infrastructure, and intellectual property—the five "Is" of open innovation. To be sure, there has always been informal knowledge leakage, but the shift to OI means that knowledge leakage should be formalized, increased, tracked, and in general turned into a core business operation. Indeed, it should not be thought of as "leakage," but as something more like an intake/outtake operation.

As there is no generally accepted definition of "knowledge" itself, "information" may be a better starting point. We can make an approximation by looking at three classes of knowledge-embedded products and how those products move: text, tools, and data. Though broad, these classes can allow us to see how the five requirements map against knowledge flow in a rough fashion, and provide some clues for how a practitioner might move to a purposeful knowledge flow business process.

Information flow is the goal of OI, but the incentives and institutional culture inside most business trend against openness. Non-disclosure agreements are standard, and there are often punishments for disclosure (not to mention that an early disclosure can foreclose the chance to file a later patent). Corporate firewalls and policies often block employees from blogging, editing wikis, or participating in typical "crowdsourced" knowledge exchange projects. In a traditional business model, this makes sense—why pay an employee to work on something else? But in the OI world, this type of participation can create the sorts of personal or technical synergies that lead to a product spinout instead of a research project cancellation, or to the identification of a promising new technology for acquisition that was "under the radar" to anyone not working as part of the online community of practice.

This attractive potential for business—the real promise of OI—has led quite a few companies to embrace its theories and attempt to implement it. However, the road to implementation of OI is a complex one. Even if the information, incentives, and institutional culture can be turned around toward an open default setting, the lack of robust knowledge-flow infrastructure can combine with the lack of legal standardization around knowledge and intellectual property rights to create resistance to OI. Where we see the success of OI, we see the existence of public systemic support for knowledge flow, and we see standardized intellectual property terms guiding the default knowledge transactions.

A good example of the five "Is" coming together for inflow and outflow is open source software as a corporate enterprise priority. IBM, for example, pays employees to work on open source projects, because their participation yields many other benefits —the perceived strength of their presence adds credibility to the overall Linux space, creates incentives for outside programmers to fix IBM's bugs (because they are everyone's bugs), and even creates a market for individuals to feature their work in hopes of landing a job at IBM. Red Hat, which runs its own flavor of Linux, makes similar investments and reaps similar benefits.

But the software world is unique in many ways. There is an enormous ecosystem of free, or nearly free, infrastructure around open source software: of code repositories and mailing list software, code versioning systems, and more that make it easy to start and maintain an open source project. There is an enormous information flow, and an enormous information stock residing on the web in searchable archives to guide new programmers and users alike. There are so many programmers in the world now that the incentives of any one individual don't matter as much—incentives can be anything from being paid by IBM to a programmer simply scratching an itch for her own fulfillment, and recontributing the code to the commons. And everything is knit together by a set of "open source copyright licenses" that guarantee the public nature of the work remains public.

However, this same ecosystem does not serve the non-software knowledge transfer world nearly as effectively. Rather than being structured into programming objects, and being composed in formal languages that machines can execute, more traditional human knowledge is unstructured, loose, free text. It is shared across multiple forms of contact from email to blogs to wikis to Microsoft Word to the PDF. Knowledge-as-text is rarely collected into centralized online knowledge repositories (with the notable exception of certain scientific discipline-specific databases of scholarly papers) for easy discovery and use, and there is a major incentive for authors inside firms to make sure their knowledge-as-text doesn't escape accidentally. Indeed, many corporations require emails to include "signatures" at their base requesting immediate destruction or return of the email if accidentally sent to the wrong person. And should the knowledge-as-text be released intentionally by the firm for collection into online systems, that firm should attach a liberal copyright permission such as a Creative Commons license.[1] Absent this, the next user is required to assume she has no rights to copy and distribute. Thus, the purposeful outflow of knowledge faces some real barriers to overcome.

The open source software example also manages inflow of information comparatively easily. The mailing lists alert all programmers to new fixes, new problems, new code. But for a knowledge worker in biotech, for example, keeping up with the literature and internal reading is burden enough—some genes generate well over 1,000 papers per year—and there is no meaningful infrastructure to move the information into either individual or corporate knowledge flows. There is some nascent use of discipline-specific web 2.0 efforts in some industries, as social networks like *2Degrees* have sprung up to increase knowledge flow among sustainability experts across corporate sectors, akin to the way that scholarly societies function to spread knowledge in academia as an adjunct to publications. As non-software efforts begin to scale, each will need to address the issues of infrastructure and intellectual property to replicate the success in open source software.

Moving data and tools, the other two kinds of knowledge-embedded products, turns out to be even more complex. Many kinds of data require an enormous investment of time on behalf of the firm to curate and make comprehensible— especially in disciplines like biology. Sharing data as an OI practice really depends on the kinds of data that are to be shared. "Simple" data like GPS data, or raw measurements gathered by sensors, tend to be more comprehensible by the external world and thus more effective from a sharing perspective. Data are also subject to a wide variety of intellectual property rights depending on national jurisdictions, which can make the reuse and integration of data deeply complex. It is far harder to create a simple, scalable, "open" license for international data flow, because data are subject to so many locally varying constraints country by country.

Tools, on the other hand, are subject to a totally orthogonal set of pressures, from patents to trade secrets to multiple ownership, which can make sharing very complex. Tools are often highly resource-consuming in development compared to text and data. And protection in a company's core business space can often result in a default position of protection everywhere, even if there is real potential for revenues outside the core business space. Moving text and data about the tools is a first step toward gaining ideas on how to repurpose technology developed in one business field to another one, allowing the external world to ideate new uses for old technology. Once that happens, another key will be making sure that the intellectual property rights system facilitates the licensing transaction on tools—the Creative Commons materials transfer and patent license projects present early steps in this direction.

Second Condition: A Market Capacity to Support Innovation

Chesbrough's second condition is that the external market must have the capacity to support innovation—and indeed, that the open innovation firm may need to invest in increasing the capacity of the external market to innovate.

This idea of the external market's "capacity to innovate" is essential to understand the assumptions behind OI, and to know where the immediate opportunities might be versus where longer-term investment might be required. Software provides an excellent example of a place where the external market has enormous capacity to innovate, and thus a good lesson for immediate implementation of OI. There are tens upon tens of thousands of programmers around the world, with access to remarkably powerful (yet cheap or free) toolkits, high bandwidth Internet access, robust programming languages, cloud storage, and more.

This means that entire software firms can run on outsourced teams, or simply leverage the infrastructure to maintain small internal project teams. The external market here is that swath of programmers. And atop this market, there is a very efficient marketplace to access those programmers. One can hire an outsourced firm, run a programming contest, or engage with programmers outside a firm or organization through any number of methods, all mediated by free/libre open source software licenses approved by the Open Source Initiative. It's easy to do open innovation in software—it just takes some willpower to rewire the way the firm thinks, because the external market is already capable of helping.

Now contrast the external support available for software with that available to the pharmaceutical industry. There are not very many biologists or medicinal chemists around the world, and most of them are fully employed. They work on systems that are deeply non-standard (cells, bodies, drugs), without robust and commonly accepted programming languages, and their toolkits are remarkably expensive. And the knowledge that is created inside a pharmaceutical company doesn't have a standardized legal way to be shared with the external market that is compatible with the business models of the industry. So the capacity of the external world to innovate is low in comparison to software.

The five "Is" are relevant here as well. If the external world lacks enough information about the firm's work, it is unlikely that an external collaborator will create value for the firm. If the firm works in a field smaller than software (which is most fields) then the number of potential collaborators is low, and the issue of incentives in the external market must be addressed. If there are no institutions in the external market (either for profit or not) that connect firms and innovators together, then the capacity of the market to innovate drops. And if the infrastructure and intellectual property rights systems are not tuned for openness, then the firm is unlikely to reap benefits from anything the external market might create.

We have addressed the first "I" already by looking at information outflow from the firm. We can turn to the issue of incentives next. If we draw the lesson too tightly from open source software we can be guilty of "survivor bias."[2] Indeed, software may well be an outlier. Thus, a firm hoping to move into OI may want to consider investing directly in the creation of incentives via prize models—and there is a growing set of intermediate companies which facilitate precisely that function. InnoCentive is one of the better-known "challenge" companies, offering either for- or non-profit firms the service of connecting to a large network of individual or corporate innovators hoping to win cash prizes for solving problems.

This contest model has created some prominent successes. One of the best documented is the Goldcorp Challenge—when mining company Goldcorp published geological data on a supposedly dying mine, offering $575,000 in total prizes to competitors with the best ideas, products, processes, and locations. More than 1,000 users worldwide competed, suggesting over 100 sites to look for gold in the mine. Eighty percent of the ideas worked, yielding more than 8,000,000 ounces of gold—nine and a half billion U.S. dollars by early 2010.

The Goldcorp story is so well known because it is so dramatic. By making an outflow of knowledge—data—to the web, Goldcorp was investing in the capacity of the external market, to which it then added the incentive of prize money. This combination of incentive and information was the key to the contest's success. But the vast majority of successful OI cases are more low-key, as evidenced by HP Labs' Open Innovation Office, which facilitates and funds external market collaboration with HP Labs scientists by simply requesting proposals for solutions to posed problems. Again, we see the pattern of bringing in external parties through a process with funding incentives, which also has the side effect of bringing many ideas into the firm through the funding process (whether or not any given idea is funded).

Goldcorp and HP Labs offer two ends of the spectrum for investing in the external capacity of the market to innovate. Goldcorp's data prospectors didn't need much more than an incentive—the prize—and their existing computational technologies. Goldcorp's goal was simply to get some new ideas and test them. HP Labs are looking for more meaningful, deep collaborations around ideas and the people who have them, so their infrastructure to increase the external capacity to help is more bureaucratic in nature, involving an actual new business unit. Other companies simply outsource the project to an external competition platform company like Inno-Centive, which performs a vital ecosystem function by connecting networks of "solvers" with "seekers" looking for answers to questions. A big part of investing in the external capacity of the market to innovate at a specific problem or task is the investment in the incentives of the external market to solve that problem or complete that task.

Technical and legal standards offer another dimension along which to measure the external capacity of a given market. Standards create a level playing field between large players and small players, and prevent "lock-in" to a proprietary set of tools and technology. Standards in network connection and document markup gave us the Internet and the web, both of which facilitate knowledge flow and distribution as well as radically increasing the total number of potential innovators with enough infrastructure to contribute to any given contest or task. Markets where the knowledge flows along proprietary formats or other systems are less likely to facilitate open innovation ecosystems (unless, of course, a format achieves a network effect and becomes a de facto monopoly—like Microsoft Word—which appears to be the primary goal for most web 2.0 businesses). Standards also radically lower transaction costs in the open intellectual property space, which is at least part of the reason for the widespread adoption of a small number of open source software licenses and the explosion of usage of the Creative Commons legal suite—the cost of licenses and legal tools drops as those tools become standard operating procedures, and as their providers become trusted members of the innovation ecosystem.

Third Condition: Value Capture in an Innovation Ecosystem

The third key element in Chesbrough's theory is that the business model is central to the capture of value in open innovation. Traditional business models often capture value by blocking the key element of open innovation, knowledge flow, and so find it difficult to turn the potential of OI into realized revenues. Indeed, some business models lead to institutional inertia, and an inability to recognize that open innovation is happening and can help drive profits. Companies can even go to the step of suing their suppliers, users, and customers, which is about as far from open innovation as possible.

In Chesbrough's thinking, a business model performs two key functions. First, it creates value through activities that deliver services or products to users. Second, it captures value by maintaining a competitive advantage. Open business models are those that divide up the "innovation labor" in these two functions.

An open business model differs from a traditional one in that intellectual property and knowledge control are not at the heart of value creation and capture. Companies like Qualcomm that operate successful open business models work with their former competitors, licensing their once tightly held intellectual property broadly, and using feedback loops to bring improvements to that IP back into their own design cycles. In practice, we find this principle applied in a variety of models: Best Buy makes corporate venture capital investments, Eli Lilly creates joint ventures and spins out innovation companies like InnoCentive, HP runs the HP Labs, Microsoft Research releases open source software for science and education. In each of them, however, there is a commitment to using the outside world to create value inside the company, by making something public that used to be private—whether money, knowledge, or intellectual property.

The biotechnology industry is a very good place to observe the core processes behind open innovation in action. There is enormous informal knowledge flow among scientists at their scholarly conferences, via journal publication, and more and more, via research blogging. Companies regularly position themselves into platform technology provider roles as one element of strategy, while continuing to use their platform and others' in the service of actual R&D for new drugs. There is regular and ongoing acquisition activity, which in its own way is a form of open innovation. However, we hesitate to name the industry as truly practicing OI, because the transaction costs associated with most of the knowledge flow are massive.

Here are a few examples. First, accessing the scholarly literature—a key source of trusted knowledge—is prohibitively expensive for most startups. Individual articles cost $25 or more, and annual subscriptions run into the tens of thousands. Subscribers lack the right to perform novel computational methods (like "text mining") against the literature as well (intellectual property rights interfering with information again). Open Access, a political response to the impact on innovation of closed scholarly journals, is addressing this problem, and now all U.S. NIH-funded research will be online, free of charge within 12 months of its publication. This creates an information infrastructure for open innovation in biomedicine.

Second, the transfer of data between companies lacks real infrastructure and standards, forcing significant and repetitive human intervention to perform curation, annotation, and integration on a deal by deal basis. The public infrastructure to store data is robust, but not to convert it into knowledge. The Semantic Web holds real promise to create a linked web of data like we have for documents, and projects like the Neurocommons aim to create open source knowledge management tools to standardize the integration and reuse of public databases.

Third, the transaction costs around tools are driven by traditional business models focused on exclusive or punitively priced patent licensing. This is driven in part by the regulatory environment (the FDA approval process can take years and cost hundreds of millions of dollars) and in part by the high failure rate of discovery (one winning patent must pay off thousands of dead ends)—but it has the unintended consequence of stifling widespread adoption of OI.

THREE EARLY DIFFICULTIES OF OI

The loud success of GoldCorp aside, systemic adoption and implementation of OI has been rough sledding. While many companies noted elsewhere in this chapter have created offices of OI, or OI initiatives, the ability to successfully use the principles of open innovation to regularly increase returns on investment is still rare. It is still far too early to make authoritative statements as to why this is the case, but some trends are emerging. We'll use the GreenXchange[3] as our case study here, because it offers some lessons that apply broadly to emerging OI across sectors.

First Difficulty

There is an established and significant inertia inside business to changing the way that knowledge flows. The modern corporation has an immune system of sorts that keeps useful knowledge inside the walls—that's where the value gets captured in the traditional business model, by having a set of systems that recognize a useful new idea, nurture it, and then filter the set of such ideas across the enterprise into product development and eventually marketing.

OI is a radical disruptor to that immune system. It is such an appealing idea that many executives in a company embrace it, but run straight into a set of interlocking resistors, none of which was designed with OI in mind (either for or against) but have the impact of slowing down the change agent. With GreenXchange, this was as simple a matter as having one business unit inside a large company tasked with the sustainability imperative (in most of the partner companies, Corporate and Social

Responsibility (CSR) groups) but another business unit tasked with product develop-ment and intellectual property protection (and thus the patent lawyers).

While the CSR units might want to share knowledge with their counterparts, if that knowledge touches on product design and development, the other business units are designed to spring into action to protect it. In one case, an interested company identified a technology for air conditioning and cooling that they had patented, but which was not part of the company's core business. The OI advocates thought that this technology, if shared, could lead to a lower unit cost for the technology if adopted across that company's business sector, and potentially even lead to licensing revenues —but only if broadly licensed at a low unit cost. Its value would go up if made open. However, the corporate reaction to this idea was 180 degrees opposite from open innovation. If the patented technology is potentially valuable, the owners reasoned, then we should find an exclusive licensee and use traditional systems to do so. The mere identification of the technology's potential value triggered a protection response.

Second Difficulty

The second problem that the GreenXchange illustrates is that sharing knowledge is expensive and complex. Nike, a company deeply committed to OI, was the first charter member to sift its patent portfolio for technologies that could be openly licensed, and quickly settled on an environmentally preferred rubber (EPR) process that lowers the petroleum needed to make rubber. This is a process that can help other shoe com-panies, and anyone else who makes rubber—which is a lot of companies—but it's not something Nike sells at the shoe store. Some early academic studies from graduate students at the University of California at Berkeley estimated that the economic impact just in India's footwear industry of implementing the EPR process could be $1 million or more per year in savings, on top of the environmental benefit. It's a perfect candidate for OI.

Nike made an early decision to license EPR widely, at no cost, asking only for notice of use and if any improvements were made and patented that those improve-ments themselves be shared back to Nike. But when the first public announcement was made, the inventor who developed EPR immediately became worried and contacted Nike senior management: if someone licensed the patent and then didn't implement the technology accurately, the environmental and economic benefits would not be realized, and indeed, might be worse than the status quo.

Nike and the GreenXchange organization swung into action, developing a set of materials and hosting a "collaboratory" for companies that wanted to use EPR. But it demonstrates that simply licensing the patent openly wasn't enough to achieve true OI—the knowledge transfer process had to be human mediated, and carefully monitored. And it's also worth noting that the portfolio itself had to be examined by internal experts, meaning the senior management at Nike had to buy into a diversion of resources from existing projects to the search for projects that could be openly shared.

Third Difficulty

The third problem builds from the second. It turns out that for many industrial sectors sharing knowledge, at least for now, is not a simple process. This is in real contrast to digital industries built on copyright, in particular software, where "ship it or share it" has become a mantra and the advent of Free/Libre and Open Source Software (FLOSS) has turned the entire sector into one populated with open innovation models.

But lots of the actionable knowledge in software is quite literally encoded. One's software code either compiles or it doesn't. Software is written in formal languages designed by people to make computers perform preset actions, and there is enough normalization of software programmers around a core set of languages that lots of software can work with lots of other software regardless of author. Software is also subject to organizational designs and hierarchy that build on infrastructure—code databases like sourceforge.com, mailing lists to coordinate priorities, and so on— that exist outside the modern software enterprise, and thus do not trigger those corporate immune responses to knowledge sharing.

We don't yet have that infrastructure for knowledge transfer in most industrial sectors. Non-software knowledge is encoded in office documents, in slide decks, in the headers of spreadsheets, in patent applications—if it's encoded at all. Often it's tacit knowledge held by the workforce themselves, never documented, and transferred via artisanal methods like conference attendance and water-cooler conversations. Social media hold promise as virtualized versions of these artisanal methods but as yet have not made significant knowledge transfer inroads.

THE LESSON: THINK LIKE A DESIGNER

So what lessons does the early experience on OI hold for a practitioner? Again, it's too early to be definitive—we are all still learning—but the importance of design is the clearest lesson. The vast majority of the problems we've encountered in OI to date stem from the basic reality that the implementations of OI exist inside systems that were designed for closed innovation. We need to take a "design thinking" approach to the ecosystems in which we innovate, both inside and outside the enterprise, if we're to see OI work in practice as well as it is capable of working in theory. It's also worth noting that Chesbrough alludes to this in his early definitions—the purposeful inflow and outflow of knowledge are most valuable when there's an external ecosystem that can actually make use of it.

The primary lesson is to design for this inflow and outflow (I/O) of knowledge. Part of designing for knowledge I/O is to be practical: use existing technical standards and formats so that external knowledge workers don't have to perform complex transformations simply to use the knowledge you're making inside the enterprise. This works for the more traditional forms of knowledge that would need to accompany a technology transfer process via open, or any other, process.

Innovators designing knowledge I/O systems should also consider information that is known prior to its capture in documents. Knowledge is built on top of data—but data are usually nowhere near knowledge itself. And we're now at a point where the collection of raw data is becoming so effortless that the problem is learning what to keep, what to throw away, and how to use the data we can collect in a way that creates capturable value. Designing the way that we collect data, so that the data emerges from the collection process in a useful way, is perhaps the single most important step that can be taken to facilitate downstream OI. The vast majority of the data that *can* be collected will be of use to someone, somewhere, but that use will remain theoretical unless the data are quickly and easily reusable.

The last part of knowledge I/O design concerns legal issues and property rights. Our current systems default to protectionism, as noted above. But even going "open" can be complicated. Transferring data, or intermediate "intellectual capital," often doesn't include the sorts of binding downstream sharing arrangements that we associate with software and with cultural objects (like those under a Creative Commons Attribution-ShareAlike license), because the laws we have don't function the same way for data and intellectual capital that they do for copyrights, patents, and trademarks. Designing systems that encourage outflow of knowledge, or at a minimum don't add friction to the decision to outflow knowledge, is essential practice.

GETTING STARTED WITH OI

There are dozens of ways that a firm or organization might begin to experiment with open innovation or open systems more generally. But there is one simple first step: make a commitment to sharing knowledge. Sharing knowledge, moving knowledge from place to place, is at the core of open innovation. There are low-friction and high-friction ways to share knowledge, legally and technically, but without an explicit commitment to sharing, attempts at open innovation will almost always hit a ceiling.

One way to get started is to examine the company's knowledge portfolio and see what assets are being used, or which assets are being under used (this is known in software as the "ship it or share it" philosophy, and is endorsed even by more traditional software companies like Microsoft). Those assets can be made available via a standard system like GreenXchange. Another way is to engage in contests via a company like InnoCentive, or to open an office of Open Innovation and call for proposals like HP. Even forming a corporate venture capital wing is in its own way a form of open innovation, although one with extremely high costs and friction.

But there is a hard lesson of the open world, one learned time and again in software and culture. Going partway, without making the commitment to sharing, without making the commitment to participation in the external market's capacity, rarely brings the yields one hopes for when adopting "open." There's an apocryphal saying that going "half open" is like half learning to break a board with your head in karate—you don't break the board, and you get a terrible headache—and if you publicized the attempt, you get embarrassed to boot. Experimenting with open innovation is going to take time, savvy, market understanding, and an external market to work with, but can yield significant results and return if you're willing to make the commitment.

NOTES

1.   To learn more, visit http://creativecommons.org/licenses.
2.   From Wikipedia: http://en.wikipedia.org/wiki/Survivorship_bias: survivorship bias is the logical error of concentrating on the people or things that "survived" some process and inadvertently overlooking those that didn't because of their lack of visibility. This can lead to false conclusions in several different ways. The survivors may literally be people, as in a medical study, or could be companies or research subjects or applicants for a job, or anything that must make it past some selection process to be considered further. Survivorship bias can lead to overly optimistic beliefs because failures are ignored, such as when companies that no longer exist are excluded from analyses of financial performance. It can also lead to the false belief that the successes in a group have some special property, rather than being just lucky.
3.   The GreenXchange provides a standardized patent license structure, whereby asset holders can control what levels and to whom their intellectual assets are available. Subsequently, those in search of new technologies have easy and direct access for licensing assets that meets their needs and obtaining direct contact with the asset holder. The license structure that makes this all happen provides a simple protocol of three options—research non-exempt, standard, and standard-PLUS—that define approved usage in a straightforward way, mitigating the traditionally expensive and drawn-out intellectual property negotiations. In addition, the GreenXchange provides a web-based network system necessary for facilitating effective intellectual asset exchange and collaboration. A select group of vetted partners have been assembled to provide services ranging from collaboration software to access to an online community of sustainable experts from around the world (http://greenxchange.cc).

Chapter 7

The Uses and Risks of Open Innovation

JAMES A. EUCHNER

INTRODUCTION

OPEN INNOVATION is a broad term. It encompasses everything from Procter & Gamble's *Connect + Develop* program, to major open-source software initiatives, and an increasing number of variants in between. The approaches all have in common the notion that innovation can be accelerated if companies break down the traditional boundaries of the corporation so that "valuable ideas can come from inside or outside the company, and can go to market from inside or outside the company, as well" (Chesbrough 2003). They differ in the degree to which this opening up happens within the traditional business model or moves beyond it and begins to shape the notion of the corporation itself.

Current approaches to open innovation can be characterized in two general categories: *open-boundary innovation* and *open-source innovation* (Euchner 2010a). *Open-boundary innovation* describes initiatives, like those advocated by Chesbrough, that are designed to source new technology and concepts broadly, seeking the seeds of the next innovation both within and outside of the corporate firewall (Slowinski 2010). Control of the innovation process itself remains within the firm, which defines priorities, chooses how to source the innovations to support them, selects providers, and integrates resulting developments into its product roadmap. Open-boundary innovation stretches the role of R&D in important ways, but it operates within the current management paradigm.

Open-source innovation, by contrast, is a more radical model that challenges fundamental assumptions about the nature of the business. At its roots, it views the source of much innovation as originating in the collective knowledge and motivation of users. In an open-source initiative, a large, and largely anonymous, community of users and innovators not only generates ideas but develops products, as well. Because community members are the source of innovation, they also govern its process and benefit from its results. It is users, acting both individually and as a community, who decide what gets worked on. Open innovation in this context means open governance and open direction, and so moves beyond the current business model.

Open source is increasingly important in the development of everything from software to prosthetics, from sporting equipment to bio-engineering. Although it emerges from similar roots, it is based on an entirely different management paradigm than open-boundary innovation. But whatever risks such new paradigms might hold, established companies ignore open-source innovation at their peril. Economic research indicates that open-source innovation may dominate corporate innovation in a steadily increasing number of fields as the costs of communication and collaboration continue to fall (Baldwin and von Hippel 2009).

One of the central differences between open-boundary and open-source innovation concerns the understanding and management of intellectual property (IP). In open-boundary innovation, control of IP remains a critical part of the management model. In the open-source model, there is no owned IP. Anyone can freely access, use, modify, and build upon the base IP.

Open-boundary innovation is important because it can accelerate the process of innovation within firms. Open-source innovation is important for more fundamental reasons:

1. It can radically change the economics of innovation by redistributing its costs and benefits.
2. It can shift the basis for competitive advantage in an industry by creating competing business models in some circumstances.
3. As a result, it may challenge the very role of the corporation in innovation.

These shifts offer both opportunities and risks for corporations.

DEFINING CHARACTERISTICS OF OPEN INNOVATION

The models of open innovation discussed above—open-boundary innovation and open-source innovation—embrace to differing degrees the possibilities and risks of being open. Far more than mere differences in degree, however, the differences between open-boundary and open-source approaches reflect starkly different assumptions about innovation itself. Assumptions about two key parameters can be used to characterize variants of open innovation:

1. The *ownership* of innovation. In open-boundary innovation, the corporation retains ownership of the intellectual property (IP) that has been developed. IP is presumed to be critical to competitive advantage. By contrast, in open-source innovation, IP (patents, code, documentation) is shared and open to all. The underlying assumption is that openness accelerates innovation.
2. The *locus of control* of innovation. In open-boundary innovation, a corporate entity makes choices about the goals of an innovation initiative and the resources to apply against those goals. This is considered essential to effective management

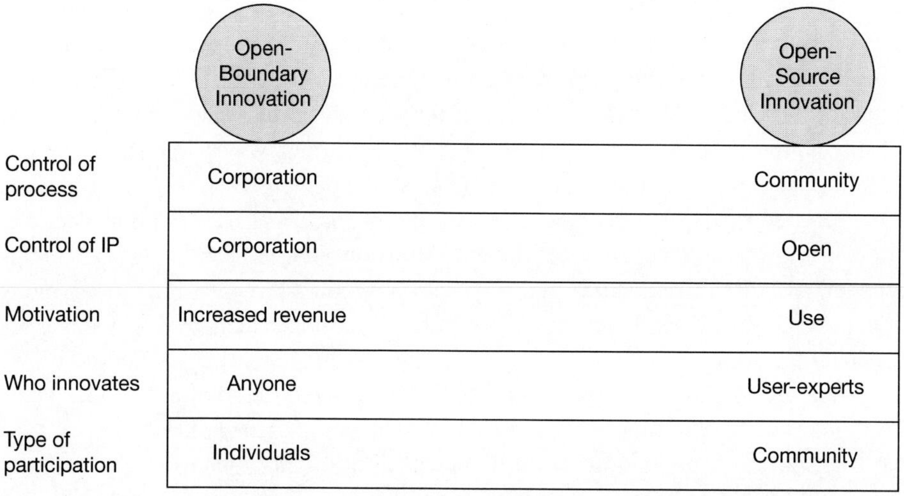

	Open-Boundary Innovation	Open-Source Innovation
Control of process	Corporation	Community
Control of IP	Corporation	Open
Motivation	Increased revenue	Use
Who innovates	Anyone	User-experts
Type of participation	Individuals	Community

Figure 7.1. Open Innovation Continuum

of the firm. In open-source innovation, on the other hand, the locus of control resides in a community of users (although corporate entities may prosper from the community's decisions and activities). In general, the contributors in open-boundary innovation are agents of the corporation, even if they are outside its boundaries, with all the implications of control that come with agency. In open-source innovation, the contributors are generally volunteers who act on their own behalf outside of the boundaries of the corporation.

Open-boundary innovation, then, generally combines a motivation to profit through the *sale* of an innovation with corporate control of the innovation process. Open-source innovation, on the other hand, usually combines the motivation to profit through the *use* of an innovation with distributed control of its evolution. There are exceptions—a firm seeking to profit from innovation may encourage an open-source movement as a competitive weapon against a dominant provider. Alternatively, a firm seeking to control the innovation process may relinquish control of some IP in order to enable standards that will benefit its industry. But in most cases, open innovation fits into one of these categories.

Figure 7.1 shows open-boundary and open-source innovation on an "open inno-vation continuum." At the left of the figure, open-boundary innovation is characterized by corporate control of both the process and the intellectual property, while open-source innovation, on the right, cedes control of both to the community. Though both open-boundary and open-source innovation leverage resources outside the firm, it is the community ethic that drives open-source innovation and the profit motive that drives open-boundary innovation. In between, a wide range of variants can be found.

THE EVOLUTION OF OPEN INNOVATION

Users have always innovated—both as individuals and as members of communities. Two decades ago, von Hippel detailed in *The Sources of Innovation* how users in many industries have been the dominant source of functionally novel innovations (von Hippel 1988). He found, for example, that 90 percent of functionally new innovations in the scientific instruments industry came from users, and demonstrated this phenomenon across a wide range of industries, especially those for which user requirements are difficult to express. Recently, he documented the prevalence of user innovation in the economy of Britain. That study indicated that users, in aggregate, may invest more in innovating than the companies that provide the basic products that they buy (von Hippel et al. 2010).

Corporations have often monetized the innovations pioneered by users: packaging them, improving them, supporting them and selling them, often without even realizing the true source of the innovation itself. Von Hippel and his colleagues showed how the process could be made systematic, in an approach that they referred to as the "lead user method" (Churchill et al. 2009; Eisenberg 2011). The lead users identified in the early studies often had both a need (as a user) and a special expertise (from their professional life). For example, an aerospace engineer who goes parasailing as a hobby might contribute to new aerodynamic designs for the parasails. Or, consider a bike-racing chiropractor who might innovate in shock absorption for mountain bikes (to take two examples cited by von Hippel 2005).

Although the lead user method was initially driven by the identification of users at the leading edge of a market need, over time it began to tap into a broader source of expertise. The method evolved to seek out expert users in analogous industries that had an intense need for an attribute of interest. Companies applying the lead user method, including 3M, Bell Atlantic, Nortel, and Pitney Bowes, found users who had solved a problem in one industry and brought the solution into their own industry. At Bell Atlantic, for example, the company sought to improve the productivity of its field technicians by equipping them with a lightweight and rugged testing device with a simple and engaging user interface. Bell Atlantic found the expertise necessary to achieve its objective of "lightweight and rugged" in expert mountain climbers. The company found the expertise needed for an "engaging user interface" in video games. In this way, the lead user method evolved from users to user-experts, and from there broadened to experts in attributes, regardless of industry. The identification of lead users was also a harbinger of open-source innovation communities. As the costs of communication have declined, it has become increasingly easy for those with a passionate interest in an area to connect with like-minded individuals and work together on innovations that matter to them.

Chesbrough expanded and popularized the open-boundary approach to innovation for corporations with his book, *Open Innovation*, in which he contrasted the open innovation paradigm with the traditional closed innovation model based on the captive R&D laboratory. Chesbrough's work encouraged companies to create porous innovation pipelines and to become more aggressive about licensing technology both in and out: working with start-up companies, spinning out concepts that don't fit with the core business, and partnering with other organizations to produce innovations. At their roots, the methods all involve search and matchmaking. They have created value for firms as diverse as Procter & Gamble and General Electric, which have used open innovation for an increasing fraction of their new product development efforts.

Open-boundary innovation has been accompanied by the emergence of a range of innovation intermediaries to facilitate the process, making it faster, more efficient and productive. Typically, these intermediaries connect a "seeker" of a solution with a network of potential "solvers." Open innovation intermediaries help their clients to frame problems in ways that are clear and likely to be productive; develop agreements to assure intellectual property rights for the "seekers"; and manage the match-making process. A wide variety of such intermediaries have made the search process more efficient. These include: technical solver communities, such as *InnoCentive*, that connect hard problems with people who might have the expertise to solve them; technology marketplaces, such as *yet2.com*, that connect companies seeking to out-license technologies to potential licensees in new markets; two-sided marketplaces, such as *NineSigma*, that seek to build a rich community of both solvers and seekers; and value-added intermediaries, such as *Gen3 Partners*, that provide methodologies for attacking and framing problems along with access to proprietary networks of solvers. Intermediaries have continued to evolve; the field now includes firms that help run innovation contests (such as the X-Prize Foundation) and intermediaries to help individual entrepreneurs (like eventys, which hosts "Everyday Edisons" on PBS).

All of these open-boundary innovation approaches operate *within the business model* of the controlling/sponsoring company. That company controls the innovation process, the definition of the problem, and the resulting IP. The solvers are rewarded financially, but do not otherwise participate in the success of the innovation.

Online technologies have enabled not only the creation of innovation inter-mediaries, but the emergence of vibrant innovation communities, as well. Although communities have always been a part of innovation, online networks have made it very easy to create places where people can connect with others with similar interests to form virtual communities. Inevitably, these communities have moved from support and information sharing to innovation. Along the way, they created a whole new form of business organization, the open-source entity.

Open-source software is the original and most widely known form of open-source innovation. There are currently hundreds of active open-source initiatives in progress, including major platforms like Apache, the web server used to support 80 percent of web pages; Linux, which competes with the Windows and Mac OS operating systems; and the Android operating system, which is at the core of a widening array of mobile phones. Open-source innovation has moved well beyond software, however. Von Hippel has documented open-source communities in prosthetics, three-dimensional printing, and a variety of sporting equipment industries, from parasailing to rodeo kayaking. In the open-source hardware fields, designs created by community members are made freely available online where anyone can use them, innovate around them, and contribute to their evolution.

CORPORATE RESPONSES TO OPEN INNOVATION

Open innovation processes continue to evolve, and so coherent strategies for responding to their threats and opportunities are still emerging. The most effective response depends very much on the corporate and industry context.

Open-Boundary Innovation: Leveraging Capabilities within the Business Model

Open-boundary innovation initiatives are prevalent in the corporate United States today, spurred in part by the widely reported success of the *Connect + Develop* program at Procter & Gamble (Lafley and Charan 2008) and the active marketing efforts of innovation intermediaries. If your competitors adopt a well-conceived and managed open-boundary innovation and you do not, they are likely to gain the advantage in cycle speed, scope of opportunity, and cost. Online networks and the emergence of innovation intermediaries have made open-boundary innovation easier, but effective adoption requires a systematic program approach and a conscious effort to build the capability.

The type of open-boundary innovation appropriate to a given business context depends both on the assets the company can effectively leverage and on its goals. The most prominent examples of open-boundary innovation today leverage the *market channels* that a corporation has established for reaching its customers. Companies like P&G, General Mills, and Johnson & Johnson have well-developed channel capabilities for which open-boundary innovation is a good complement. If a new product can be identified through any means, within the corporation or beyond its boundaries, these companies can leverage well-developed and reliable engines for testing, branding, marketing, and pulling it through their channels.

Another common asset leveraged by corporations in open-boundary innovation is the *customer base*. Traditionally, firms have attempted to tap into their existing customers for insights into new offerings through user groups, sales outreach, and formal "voice of the customer" approaches. It has been difficult, however, to synthesize and respond to this input. Open-boundary innovation can create a more intimate, interactive relationship with customers. The best examples require relinquishing significant control of the innovation process to the user community. For instance, Coloplast, a medical products company, nurtures an independent and open community of users who share their medical issues and collaborate to create designs to resolve them. The company provides rich tools for communication, design, collaboration, and even prototyping, and users create, share, and improve upon one another's designs (Kragh 2011).

Proprietary data offer another potential source of competitive advantage that can be leveraged through open-boundary innovation. Opening data to analysis by those beyond the walls of the firm has been famously successful for Netflix, which ran a contest to develop an algorithm to improve the quality of its movie recommendations. The prize was won by a team of experts who met and collaborated as part of the initiative. Similarly, GoldCorp opened up its geologic data to external experts in an attempt to find new deposits on its properties. Working for a prize of $500,000 the external solvers made key contributions—including a new approach to visualizing the data—that resulted in the identification of significant new deposits (Tapscott and Williams 2006).

Finally, a corporation may have a *proprietary platform* that it seeks to leverage by a controlled openness. In this model, others are encouraged to innovate on top of the platform. As long as the platform itself remains proprietary, any innovation that builds on it accrues to the advantage of the firm. Apple and its App Store (iOS), the official online application distribution system for iPad, iPhone, and iPod Touch, provide an excellent example of use of a proprietary platform in open-boundary innovation. iOS allows screened and approved application writers to offer their software for sale through the online store. The developer keeps 70 percent of the revenue, and Apple keeps the remainder. Over 80 percent of the applications are free, and the top line revenue is small, but the App Store makes the Apple devices worth much more to users, and hence adds to hardware sales.

Similarly, T-shirt company Threadless.com relies entirely on its community to submit T-shirt designs, select the ones it will sell, and purchase them. Its *proprietary platform* is its customer- and designer-friendly website. National Semiconductor has developed a suite of tools, called Workbench, to enable users to design analog devices using NatSemi as the fabricator. Its platform is not just the suite of tools, but the components and infrastructure behind them that make fulfillment possible.

These sources of open-boundary competitive advantage are listed in Table 7.1, along with the open-boundary innovation approaches each can leverage (see Text Box). Without explicitly seeking to leverage a particular advantage, a firm is not likely to succeed with open-boundary innovation. At times, combinations may be effective.

Table 7.1. Approaches to open-boundary innovation to leverage competitive advantages

Source of competitive advantage	Open-boundary innovation methods	Results	Examples
Channel/brand	Intermediaries (search)	New products	P&G, GE
Customer base	Gated communities; crowdsourcing tools	New features; improved design	Coloplast
Proprietary data	Contests	New methods; better processes	Netflix, GoldCorp
Proprietary platform	Developer/designer/ user ecosystem	Designs fulfilled through company; "long-tail" applications	Apple, Threadless

SPECIFIC TECHNIQUES FOR OPEN-BOUNDARY INNOVATION

Open-boundary innovation incorporates many techniques. Each operates within the business model of the corporation but is open to innovations and ideas coming from outside its organizational boundaries. The primary types of open-boundary innovation are:

1. *Crowdsourcing.* In crowdsourcing, a problem or issue is put to a large, often diverse collection of individuals (a crowd). These individuals provide ideas responsive to the challenge and may comment or build upon the ideas of others. Crowdsourcing is most useful for generating ideas or designs, not for developing full solutions. It works most effectively when coupled with governance approaches that funnel the ideas to those who can filter, analyze, and act on them. Companies like Pfizer and Pitney Bowes have used crowdsourcing internally to generate ideas for improving products and operations (Dahl et al. 2011). Some companies are experimenting with opening up these initiatives to customers. Crowdsourcing is least successful when it attempts to address complex and urgent problems like solutions to the Gulf Oil spill (Euchner 2010b). Although recognition of some sort is often part of a crowdsourcing initiative, rewards are usually not a major driver.

2. *Contests.* An innovation contest is similar to a crowdsourcing initiative in that it starts with a challenge to a large, diverse base of contributors. The challenge, however, is framed as a competition with a prize for the most successful solution offered. The problem itself must be well defined and its solution measurable in some way. For instance, the Netflix contest required participants to develop an algorithm that was 10 percent more effective in recommending movies to customers than the company's existing recommendation algorithms. A contest almost always involves a reward of some sort, and that reward can be substantial. In some contests, competitors submit entries confidentially; at other times, the entries are open for others to build upon.

3. *Innovation intermediaries.* The last 10 years have seen the emergence of a range of innovation intermediaries. The first of these was InnoCentive, which permitted companies to post difficult chemistry problems to a community of chemists. In theory, if the community is large enough, someone is likely to have the combination of skills that make the problem tractable. InnoCentive has since broadened its scope, and other intermediaries have emerged, each with its own approach to improve the process of matchmaking. Common elements include assistance in structuring the problem, clear management of intellectual property rights, management of

the contracting among parties, and access to a large network of potential solvers. Intermediaries differ in the nature of their networks, the scope of problems and assistance they provide to those seeking solutions, and their method of framing the problems they work on. Innovation intermediaries seem to work best in solving well-defined technical problems, although they have also been used to find new markets for a technical capability and to identify new product categories. Effective use of intermediaries requires capabilities inside the corporation for framing, reviewing, and complementing the work of the solvers.

4. *Platform innovation.* An ideal for open innovation is the development of a vibrant community of innovators who innovate using your platform. The Apple App Store for iPhones and iPads is an example of a rich developer community tied to a particular platform. Establishing such a platform is difficult. Everyone within an industry would like to be the platform; no competitor wants to cede the position to another. Even brilliant design, a loyal customer base, and a large corpus of innovations are not enough to assure that the platform will not be challenged, however. The emergence of the highly successful Android open-source mobile operating system was spawned by a desire to create a competing platform to Apple's iOS.

5. *Gated communities.* Although it is still rare, open-boundary innovation can extend to communities of users. The key issue for corporations in attempting to build such communities is relaxing control: a community will not thrive if its agenda is controlled by the corporation; it will devolve to an online user group using crowdsourcing software. Some true communities nurtured by corporate entities are beginning to emerge, however. LEGO benefits not only from online communities of enthusiastic users, like LUGNET, but also from a gated community the company created to assist with new product testing and development. Corporations have also created gated communities of software developers to share problems and solutions. Gated communities can work when the user base is highly motivated to engage and when the corporation is willing to trade control and intellectual property for engagement.

These forms of open-boundary innovation are indicated in Figure 7.2, which is an adaptation of Figure 7.1. (Note that, from a business model perspective, the first three approaches are very similar.)

Figure 7.2 shows variants of open-boundary innovation on the Open Innovation Continuum. Pure versions of open-boundary innovation include crowdsourcing, innovation contests, and the use of innovation intermediaries as matchmakers between seekers and solvers. In each of these, corporate control is a primary design factor. In the proprietary platform variant of open-boundary innovation, corporations cede some control (but gain broader acceptance) by opening up their platform so that others can innovate on top of it. Control of the platform is shared in order to achieve the objectives of more rapid innovation. Corporations cede even more control with gated communities. Though the corporation may decide who is invited to participate in a gated community and may respond to community requests according to its internal interests, successful gated communities require genuine opportunities for the community to shape direction and a corporate sponsor that is responsive to community needs. In all cases, significant intellectual property rights remain with the corporation.

	Crowdsourcing, Contests, Intermediaries	Proprietary Platform	Gated Community	Open-Source Innovation
Control of process	Corporation	Shared		Community
Control of IP	Corporation			Open
Motivation	Increased profit			Use
Who innovates	Anyone	Invited group		User-experts
Type of participation	Individuals	Invited group		Community

Figure 7.2. Open-Boundary Innovation Spectrum

Open-Source Innovation

The appropriate corporate response to open-source innovation is more difficult to define. Responding to open-source innovation will require departures from traditional business models and may include significant risks to revenues and margins. Giving away core product, relinquishing IP rights, or sharing future product directions with an independent community are difficult actions for a corporation to contemplate, but they are inherent in true open-source models. Of course, open-source innovation has advantages; it offers the potential for tighter relationships with customers, lower costs for product innovation, and faster cycle times for new products.

Departure from a well-established business mode brings with it risks that are not foreseeable. Corporate innovators and strategists contemplating an open-source initiative should therefore address four questions:

1. *Is entry into the business domain by an open-source competitor likely?* Although there are open-source communities that innovate in the domain of physical

products (non-software), the potential for disruption from an open-source model most often comes from the digital realm, where constraints of time and place are greatly reduced and the size of the potential community is very large. When important artifacts of the innovation process—design sketches, databases, software, CAD/CAM renderings—can be digitized, innovation can be opened up to a large base of distributed, diverse contributors. Although the most prominent open-source communities are in the software domain, as noted above, successful virtual communities have been established in parasailing, prosthetics, 3D printing, and even automobiles.

2.   *Is there a compelling motivation for an open-source alternative?* Open-source efforts thrive on passion, both positive and negative. A community is more likely to emerge as a result of three distinct motivations (or combinations of them): a passion for a product or activity; an emotional response to a dominant provider; or a compelling niche need that is not being addressed by mass-market solutions.

Passion-driven communities emerge from groups of people who care deeply about a product or an activity and believe that they must innovate to get what they need; these sorts of communities frequently evolve around an avocation like sporting equipment.

When a community emerges in response to a dominant provider, on the other hand, the motivation to create an alternative is generally emotional, not economic, at its core. Open Windows emerged in this way, with a community of users united around opposition to Microsoft's dominance of PC software. Similarly, the Android operating system for smart phones, sponsored by Google, was motivated by the desire to create a viable alternative to the Apple iPhone and App Store. It brought into alignment those with an ideological passion for open source and those with a business interest in competing with Apple.

Finally, an open-source community may arise from participants' drive to fill niche needs that are not (and perhaps cannot) be met within a corporation's mass-market business model. People in these communities are motivated to share their solutions to these "long-tail" opportunities (Anderson 2006) because the market for them is small.

Pure economics plays into each of these motivations for creating an open alternative, but it does not dominate any of them. The free nature of the products, however, significantly affects their use and competitive positioning.

3.   *Can the business effectively respond to a potential open-source alternative within its current business model?* Corporations can approach the potential for open-source competition by responding to its motivations and by reducing the incentives for an open-source alternative to arise. The best response for firms may be to head off open-source competition simply by being a good supplier: price fairly, provide exceptional support, and engage the user community deeply. A company can also proactively engage with and build its own user community, filling the need that might have otherwise been taken up by an independent open-source community. In this case, achieving the necessary level of intimacy will likely require letting go of some control, permitting the community to participate in

product development and perhaps even dictate the future directions of the product. Few established companies have been able to accomplish this.

4. *Can the business create a new business model that effectively leverages the open-source alternative?* A firm might even embrace the potential for open-source innovation and reshape its business model accordingly. As Eric von Hippel has noted, in some instances it may make sense for a company to get out of the innovation business altogether and reconfigure itself as the production arm of an innovation community. This is now happening in parasailing. The community of hobbyist parasailers has became so strong—including participants with aerospace, materials, and simulation skills—that its designs outperform those of any for-profit manufacturer. The new business model for manufacturers in this arena evolved into one focused on providing high-quality manufacturing of designs created by the community. This evolution away from fully integrated businesses competing on design to manufacturing firms competing on cost, service, speed, and quality is not uncommon in business history.

   Industries often start with firms combining a high degree of R&D and custom applications engineering with manufacturing; over time, they evolve into a manu-facturing role, often through the emergence of user-friendly toolkits that enable users to take over large parts of the design tasks (within the constraints of the manufacturing platform). The evolution of the application-specific integrated circuit (ASIC) market followed this evolution, as has the market for engineered plastics. Online communities may be accelerating the transition, but agile firms that are successful in making themselves the manufacturing platform of choice can remain strong even in the face of a robust open-source innovation community.

   Alternately, a firm can decide not to compete with an open-source movement but to complement it. Red Hat, which provides stable releases of Linux along with support and training, is one such example. Although Red Hat emerged from the open-source community itself, supplementing a product users could get for free with the technical support and training assistance larger users require, a firm might just as well make the strategic decision to make its proprietary offering open source. Sun Microsystems did just this with its Java programming language.

Figure 7.3 shows a "force field diagram" indicating the forces that drive and the forces that restrain the movement toward open-source innovation. At the center of the diagram is an industry's digital innovation platform, which depends on charac-teristics of the industry under consideration, but which changes over time as the industry evolves and as technology enables new capabilities.

The diagram can be used both to anticipate the potential for open-source entry and to develop strategies for responding to that possibility. As Karl Lewin noted, it is easier to create desired change by removing barriers to adoption than by increasing forces of motivation (Weisbord 1987), and many technology trends are in play which tend to reduce the barriers to open source across industries. The last decade has seen the emergence of better tools for managing collaboration (such as those provided by Collabnet), improved support for open-source alternatives (such as the technical

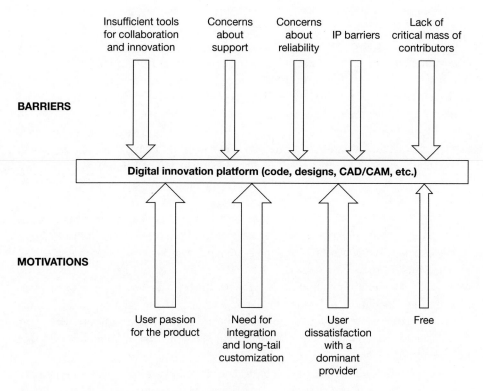

Figure 7.3. Open-Source Innovation Force Field Diagram

support Red Hat provides for Linux), new patent commons initiatives (such as the planned BIOS commons for biology), and tools for building community (such as social networking capabilities). Each of these facilitates open-source efforts and makes the emergence of open-source alternatives more likely.

The barriers to a flowering of open-source innovation are thinning. Innovators and strategists must ask if and when their industry might make the transition—and what the appropriate response might be.

CONCLUSIONS

Open innovation approaches are more than just new innovation techniques. They have the potential to shift the dynamics of competition in a wide variety of industries. As such, they are an important strategic issue. Corporate responses to date are just a harbinger of what is likely to come.

It is important that companies consider open innovation in this strategic context. Doing so will require rethinking many tenets of business: that the corporation is the source of innovation, that innovation must be directed by the corporation to be successful, that IP ownership is essential to business success—even that innovation itself is a key role of the corporation.

Assessing the proper response starts with a true understanding of the ways in which openness can add value in your industry. This requires understanding not only the potential to drive faster and broader innovation than is possible within your corporate boundaries; it requires that you see users as more than customers, but as a latent community with the potential to innovate. Corporations must ask: Is there the potential (and motivation) for users to create an open alternative to our business model? Can we nurture user communities in a way that responds to their needs within our business model, or will our business model need to be revised? Can we open our product architecture to users in a way that is meaningful to them without threatening our revenue sources? What level of intellectual property protection is likely to make sense in the future? Might our current approach work against our positioning with users?

Most businesses will start their open innovation journey by embracing open-boundary approaches in order to accelerate growth within the confines of their current business model. Astute businesses will go beyond these approaches and reevaluate their business models for an open-source world. They will seek to create platforms that allow user communities to innovate—whether through technology platforms that provide the foundation for wider innovations (such as the Android smart phone platform), customer platforms that help connect corporate innovators to user ideas (such as gated communities), or manufacturing platforms that fulfill designs created by user communities.

This evolution will be threatening to the corporate innovation structure—creating, managing, leveraging, and controlling innovation and its fruits has long been a central function of the corporation—but it is essential to truly grappling with the increasing power of online communities and user innovation.

REFERENCES

Anderson, C. (2006) *The Long Tail*. New York: Hyperion Books.

Baldwin, C. Y. and von Hippel, E. A. (2009) "Modeling a Paradigm Shift: From Producer Innovation to User and Open Collaborative Innovation." Working Paper, Cambridge, MA: MIT Sloan School of Management.

Chesbrough, H. (2003) *Open Innovation*. Boston: Harvard Business School Publishing Corporation.

Churchill, J., von Hippel, E., and Sonnack, M. (2009) Lead User Project Handbook (available online).

Dahl, A., Lawrence, J., and Pierce, J. (2011) "Building and Innovation Community," *Research-Technology Management*, Sept/Oct: 19.

Eisenberg, I. (2011) "Lead-User Research for Breakthrough Innovation," *Research-Technology Management*, Jan/Feb.

Euchner, J. (2010a) "Two Flavors of Open Innovation," *Research-Technology Management*, July/Aug: 7.

Euchner, J. (2010b) "The Limits of Crowds," *Research-Technology Management*, Sept/Oct: 7.

Kragh, P. (2011) Private communication.

Lafley, A. G. and Charan, R. (2008) *The Game Changer*. New York: Crown Business.

Slowinski, G. (2010) "Good Practices in Open Innovation," *Research-Technology Management*, Sept/Oct: 38.

Tapscott, D. and Williams, A. (2006) *Wikinomics*. New York: The Penguin Group.

von Hippel, E. (1988) *The Sources of Innovation*. New York: Oxford University Press.

von Hippel, E. (2005) *Democratizing Innovation*. Cambridge, MA: MIT Press.

von Hippel, E., Thomke, S., and Sonnack, M. (1999) "Creating Breakthroughs at 3M," *Harvard Business Review*, Sept/Oct: 47.

von Hippel, E., De Jong, J., and Flowers, S. (2010) "Comparing Business and Household Sector Innovation in Consumer Products: Findings from a Representative Study in the UK" (September 27). Available at SSRN: http://ssrn.com/abstract=1683503.

Weisbord, M. (1987) *Productive Workplaces*. San Francisco: Jossey-Bass.

Chapter 8

Entrepreneurship and Venture Capital in the Age of Collective Intelligence

ROBERT LAUBACHER

DURING THE FIRST HALF of the twentieth century, the locus of innovation was the corporate lab, housed inside the research and development departments of large enterprises like General Electric, DuPont, and AT&T (Hounshell and Smith 1988; Reich 2002). After World War II, venture capital firms came into being, which allowed entrepreneurs with promising ideas to establish start-up companies in the absence of involvement by established corporations. In recent decades, start-up companies funded by venture capitalists have been responsible for most of the key innovations in emerging sectors of the economy, most notably information technology and biotechnology (Gompers and Lerner 2001).

The semiconductor shows the transition between these two modes of innovation. The device itself was developed at Bell Labs in the early 1950s. One of the inventors, William Shockley, founded his own firm, Fairchild Semiconductor, in 1957. Arthur Rock, a New York banker, provided the initial financing. Rock was a transitional figure between the world of early twentieth-century corporate finance and the venture capital-based practices that later became prevalent. Alumni of Fairchild went on to found more than 40 Silicon Valley technology companies, and the success of Fairchild spurred the development of the first venture capital firms in the San Francisco Bay area (Florida and Kenney 1988).

With the rise of venture capital, the innovation function, for emerging industries at least, moved outside of the large corporation and instead came to be undertaken by the new venture sector, comprising decentralized, external networks of entrepreneurs, university researchers, and financiers, all linked by venture capital firms. This externalization of innovation was part of a larger trend, beginning over the latter part of the twentieth century, toward more distributed forms of business organization (Powell 1990; Malone 1997). For example, during the 1980s and 1990s, many large corporations reorganized into smaller and more autonomous business units (Bartlett and Ghoshal 1993), came to rely more extensively on far-flung supply chains (Simchi-Levi et al. 2003) and ecosystems of partners (Brandenburger and Nalebuff 1998), and increased their usage of outsourcing and offshoring (Quinn 1999).

The past decade has seen the emergence of new, even more radically distributed ways of organizing work, enabled by the global expansion of the Internet. Prominent examples include Linux, Wikipedia, and Google. In Linux and Wikipedia, volunteers from all over the world work together to develop software and write encyclopedia articles. Google is perhaps an even more interesting example, when one considers not just Google the firm, but the entire system invoked every time a person types a query into the Google search box. This system takes advantage of the efforts of everyone who creates links on the World Wide Web. Each link is an implicit judgment that a page is worth viewing, and the sum total of all the links thus represents an aggregated global judgment about what web content is of value. Google, the company, uses its crawlers to gather the content of all web links on an ongoing basis, stores this information on its servers, and parses it with clever algorithms that assess which judgments embodied in links are reliable indicators of quality. Focused portions of this ongoing collective global judgment about the quality of web content then get served up to users when they type in queries.

Systems like these, which rely on distributed groups working together, connected by the Internet, have been described by such terms as wisdom of crowds (Surowiecki 2004), peer production (Benkler 2006), wikinomics (Tapscott and Williams 2008), crowdsourcing (Howe 2009), or collective intelligence (Malone 2006).

The emergence of the venture capital sector transformed the way the innovation process worked: innovation went from being an activity that took place inside corporate research labs to a more distributed process that involved interactions between university researchers, entrepreneurs, and financiers, orchestrated by venture capitalists. Could the development of collective intelligence-based mechanisms for organizing work lead to another transformation of the innovation process? Specifically, could some or even all of the innovation activities that in recent decades have come to be undertaken by the new venture sector become the province of crowds linked via the Internet?

This chapter will consider the prospects for such a transformation by examining the potential impact of collective intelligence on: (a) entrepreneurs and their start-up companies, and (b) venture capital firms. We will use the "Collective Intelligence Genome" (Malone et al. 2010) to examine the potential overall impact of collective intelligence on start-ups and venture capital firms. First, we describe this recently developed taxonomy, which categorizes the design patterns that underlie web-enabled collective intelligence systems. Then we apply its concepts to understand the way in which collective intelligence drives the risks (and rewards) of new ventures and venture investment.

THE COLLECTIVE INTELLIGENCE GENOME

The Collective Intelligence Genome (or CI Genome) is based on analysis of more than 200 examples of collective intelligence. It maps the structure of collective intelligence systems by asking four key questions:

- *What* is being done?
- *Who* is doing it?
- *Why* are they doing it?
- *How* are they doing it?

The answers to these four questions constitute the building blocks—or genes—of the systems.

For the question, *What is being done?* there are two genes: Create and Decide. In the Create gene, the task is the development of a new artifact or part of one— lines of code in Linux, encyclopedia articles or edits to encyclopedia article in Wikipedia, videos in YouTube. In the Decide gene, the task is making a decision, and in many instances, the decision involves an evaluation of quality. The items being evaluated can exist in the physical world, such as restaurants or shops, which are the focus of sites like Yelp, or in the online world, like the ratings of buyers and sellers on eBay.

For the second question, *Who is doing it?* there are also two genes: Crowd and Hierarchy. In the Crowd gene, anyone who is a member of a particular group can choose to participate in the task. In some instances, the group includes only a select category of people. For example, in IBM's Innovation Jams, only IBM's employees and the company's customers and suppliers are allowed to participate. In other instances, anyone in the entire world who wishes to can participate. For example, any person with access to a computer with a web browser can edit Wikipedia articles. In the Hierarchy gene, the task is undertaken by a person assigned to do it by someone in a position of authority. The Hierarchy gene describes the way work typically gets assigned in most traditional business organizations.

Use of the crowd gene marks a distinguishing feature of collective intelligence systems. What is new and innovative—and has only emerged on a broad basis over the past decade, with the global diffusion of the Internet—is widespread reliance on the crowd in this way. Entrepreneurs who are seeking ways to tap into the new possibilities enabled by these emerging practices will want to think about how they might incorporate the crowd in their ventures.

For the third question, *Why are they doing it?* there are three genes: Money, Glory, and Love. Money is the mechanism used primarily in business organizations today. Glory is at work when people participate to receive recognition from peers or from other users of the system. Love covers a range of motivational factors: when people participate because they like an activity for its own sake, because they enjoy interacting with other members of an online community, or because they feel they are contributing to a cause larger than themselves. Many web-enabled collective intelligence systems rely on Glory and Love as motivational factors.

The final question, *How are they doing it?* has a different set of answers depending on whether a hierarchy or a crowd is involved—and here the genome becomes a bit complicated. When the task is undertaken by a hierarchy, the answer to this question is based on the design principles that underlie the organization. For example, organizations may group people and responsibilities according to function, product line, geography, or by using matrix structures that combine elements of each.

But when the task is undertaken by a crowd, the answer to the How? question flows from two other questions. The first is the previously asked What? question—is the task to Create or Decide? And the second is another sub-question: *Do individual members of the crowd provide independent, stand-alone contributions or do they provide interdependent contributions that get combined into a larger whole?* When contributions by members of the crowd are *independent*, each member of the crowd contributes an item that is an end product of the system. For example, in YouTube, members of the crowd submit complete videos, and these are made available, as is, to visitors of the site. When contributions are *interdependent*, each participant submits a portion of the whole, and these contributions are combined. For example, in Wikipedia, text and edits submitted by many contributors get combined in the encyclopedia articles that appear on the site.

These two dimensions of crowd tasking (create vs. decide and independent contributions vs. interdependent contributions) combine (as shown in Figure 8.1) to yield a rich variety of subsidiary genes. We explain each in turn.

When the crowd submits independent creations, the result is the Collection gene. YouTube is a well-known collection. Another prominent example is iStockPhoto, a site where photographers submit images that are made available to advertising agencies and graphic designers for use in magazines, brochures, websites, and other kinds of visual materials.

An interesting variant of the Collection is the Contest, where a subset of the submitted items is chosen and made available to customers. Threadless uses a contest model to develop designs for the T-shirts it sells. Each week, the company invites artists to submit new designs in an online contest. Customers rate the entrants, and the management team at Threadless selects a handful of them and awards each designer who submitted a winning entry a prize of several thousand dollars. Threadless then has the T-shirts produced and sells them on its website and in its retail stores.

Where each member of the crowd contributes only a part of the eventual end product we find the other group creation gene, Collaboration. When the Collaboration gene is used, the mechanism for assembling individual contributions becomes a key element of the system. In some instances, as with Linux, this assembly challenge is at least partially met through the use of a modular design framework, with well-defined interfaces governing interactions between key parts of the system. In other cases, managing the interdependencies between individual contributions is an important part of the work done by the contributors themselves. Wikipedia manages the reassembly challenge through the general principle that an article at any given time reflects a rough consensus of the interested editors. The Wikipedia community

	Independent	Interdependent
Create	Collection Contest	Collaboration
Decide	Social Network Market	Voting Averaging Consensus Prediction Market

Figure 8.1. Variations of the How Gene for Tasks Undertaken by Crowds

has also developed a set of sophisticated rules for handling situations where interested editors find it difficult to reach consensus.

We find the Individual Decision gene when each member of the crowd submits independent decisions, and these are all made available to users of the system. Links in the blogosphere are one example of the Individual Decision gene—each blogger chooses to embed links to other websites they believe might be of interest to their readers. The underlying social network of the links thus structures how a user perceives which material is of interest and value. The ask and bid prices in eBay are another example of the Individual Decision gene—the seller's reserve price and the bidders' offering prices are all individual assessments of the value of the item, and each of these assessments is made visible to any user of the site. In this instance, buying and selling activity in a market is the mechanism by which information from a number of individual decisions is provided to users of the system. Social Network and Market are thus the two genes that can be chosen in the Individual Decision category.

In the Group Decision gene, members of the crowd submit decisions that are then aggregated into an overall decision that stands for the group as a whole. An example of a Group Decision is when open source software developers use voting to determine the overall direction of the project—for example, about which of several possible features to make the top priority for future development. Each community member expresses their preference, but these preferences are then aggregated—sometimes by simple counting of votes, and sometimes by complex preferential voting algorithms—into a decision that stands for the group as a whole.

A variety of interesting mechanisms have emerged in web-based collective intelligence systems for making Group Decisions, and in the CI Genome framework, these are each classified as separate genes in their own right. These mechanisms include Voting (described above); Averaging (when the arithmetic mean of individual ratings is simply calculated); Consensus (arrived at either by social procedures, as in Wikipedia, or when the individual judgments converge above a specified statistical threshold, as in systems like NASA Clickworkers); and Prediction Markets (where members of the crowd buy and sell predictions about possible future outcomes, with

		What	Who	Why	How
Threadless	Create	T-shirt designs	Crowd	Money Love	Contest
	Decide	Which designs are best	Crowd	Love	Averaging
	Decide	Which designs to use	Management	Money	Hierarchy

Figure 8.2. Genome Map for Threadless

the resulting prices on the exchange representing the crowd's aggregate judgment about the likelihood of each potential outcome).

In practice, systems that use the Individual Decision gene often rely on quantitative metrics, such as the five-star rating system used for books by Amazon, movies by Netflix, and restaurants by Yelp. The individual ratings can then easily be aggregated, usually by averaging, into an overall group rating. In cases where it is easy to aggregate individual input to derive a group assessment, systems frequently display both the individual ratings as well as the overall group rating. Such systems thus combine both the Individual and Group Decisions.

Most collective intelligence systems are comprised of multiple activities combined in particular ways. The combination of all the building blocks, or genes, that constitute a collective intelligence system constitute its overall design pattern—or, as it is called in the framework, its genome. The genome of a system can be mapped in a diagram that shows all of the system's activities and the genes associated with them. Consider, for example, Threadless, the T-shirt company described previously that relies on its community to submit designs, select the ones it will sell . . . and then actually purchase them. This genome is illustrated in Figure 8.2.

The genome of Threadless includes three core activities:

- Create T-shirt designs, by the Crowd, for Money and Love, through a Contest;
- Decide which designs are best, by the Crowd, for Love, by Averaging;
- Decide which designs to print, by Management, for Money, by Hierarchy.

In principle, any combination of genes is possible. But certain combinations have shown themselves to be especially adaptive in certain situations. In particular, some configurations have been used extensively by start-up companies in the past decade. Others have begun to be used in ways that encroach on the traditional functions of venture capital firms.

POTENTIAL IMPACT OF COLLECTIVE INTELLIGENCE ON START-UP COMPANIES

In many contemporary start-up companies, the crowd, accessed via the Internet, is enlisted to do a key part of the work of the new venture, work that would previously have been undertaken by the start-up's employees. Start-ups rely on crowds both to create and to decide. Threadless incorporates both in its model—a crowd of designers contributes new designs and a crowd of customers helps to decide which of those designs to produce (though Threadless management makes the final decision). Threadless thus effectively enlists an online crowd to undertake its product development and market research functions.

Use of Crowd Creation in Start-Ups

For crowd creation, both the Collection and Contest gene have proven useful for start-ups. The successes of YouTube (which was acquired by Google) and iStockPhoto (which was acquired by Getty Images, a long-established provider of stock photographs) demonstrate the viability of the Collection gene.

The Contest gene has proven even more compelling, serving as the basis for a large number of new companies in a variety of domains. Among the more prominent examples are InnoCentive, which uses a contest model to solve complex scientific problems; TopCoder, which develops software using contests; Netflix, which paid a $1 million prize for an algorithm that achieved a 10 percent improvement in the effectiveness of a recommendation engine to match customers with movies; and Local Motors, a recently launched auto maker that holds contests for new car designs (Jana 2009).

Contests are by no means the exclusive province of web-enabled collective intelligence systems. Business plan competitions have long been used in universities and by venture capitalists to identify promising ideas for start-up companies. The launch of the X Prize for space travel in the 1990s, and subsequent X Prize contests in other domains—as well as the prominence on television of entertainment contests like *American Idol*—have greatly increased public awareness of the Contest gene. Prizes have a long heritage and provided the impetus for creation of some of the masterpieces of Renaissance Italy (Haines 1989), as well as scientific and engineering breakthroughs such as the development of instruments for ocean navigation in the eighteenth century and Charles Lindbergh's solo flight across the Atlantic Ocean in 1927 (X Prize Foundation 2011).

The collection and contest are attractive models for start-up companies because they have the potential to accomplish work formerly done in-house more cheaply and/or more effectively. Both the collection and the contest models effectively lower barriers to participation and can thus unleash the talents of enthusiastic amateurs who might otherwise not have had an outlet for their work.

Collections can certainly provide opportunities for a broader group of contributors than traditional structures, where typically only dedicated, credentialed professionals could previously break in. iStockPhoto accepts contributions from hobbyist photographers who do not depend on the site as a source of professional income. And exposure on YouTube has provided an outlet for many performers to get their work in front of an audience, in some cases opening up opportunities for them in the mainstream entertainment industry. A notable recent example is the pop singer Justin Bieber, who was discovered by a record producer after Bieber's mother posted videos of his performances on YouTube.

Contests can elicit significant effort from many members of the crowd, with only the best contributions being used, and thus they can potentially be quite cost effective—though this is dependent on the bounty being large enough to attract a sufficient number of contributors. And the true value of contests is often not in the number of participants but in the diversity of ideas they can produce, and in contests' ability to identify uncommon talents that are very widely distributed. The latter is a key advantage of InnoCentive, which taps a far-flung global network to solve challenging scientific and engineering problems.

To date, the Collaboration gene has been used primarily by mission-driven non-profits, as exemplified by Linux and Wikipedia, and has not been relied upon extensively by for-profit start-ups (though it has been used indirectly by companies like Red Hat, which provide services linked to open source software development projects). One difficulty associated with direct use of the Collaboration gene in a for-profit setting comes from the need to measure and reward incremental effort by crowd members who choose to contribute. In most current web-based collective intelligence systems that rely on Collaboration, many individuals contribute to the effort, with their contributions varying greatly in size and number. Developing a system that could measure and incentivize contributions at a sufficiently detailed level could be a sizeable challenge, though experiments are underway to do just that (Robb 2011).

A software development contest sponsored by Matlab has evolved a structure that combines the competitive elements of a contest with collaboration. The contest asks software developers to write code that is judged on how well it solves the problem at hand and how quickly it runs. Entries get judged at intervals and scores are made available to all contestants. Contestants are able to borrow code from other contributors whose work appears promising (Gulley 2004). This structure effectively combines the Contest and Collaboration genes, but it is enabled by the nature of the work, in particular by the fact that all contest entries can be judged quickly, using another computer program, on an ongoing basis. Creating hybrid structures that combine the Contest and Collaboration genes in less structured settings can create complexity that may be difficult to manage (Boudreau and Lakhani 2009). But this is also a promising area for potential future experimentation.

Use of Crowd-generated Decisions for Start-Ups

Managing systems that rely on collective intelligence-based crowd decisions is relatively straightforward when the crowd's input can be obtained without active consent from contributors, for example, through crawlers that mine information on the web or through the collection and storage of electronic traces left by people in the course of engaging in everyday activities on the web. Google is a good example of a firm that takes advantage of this approach. Because the Internet is accessible to anyone, Google's crawlers can readily identify and gather web links without the need for any active contribution by or consent from the people who create those links. The challenge for Google is to keep up with the constantly expanding amount of content on the web, which means its crawlers must always be checking for new links and its servers must be continually updated.

Systems that rely on active decisions from the crowd, as opposed to capturing crowd decisions automatically, face a larger challenge (see Cook (2008) on the distinction between active and passive contributions). Sometimes the collection of decisions from the crowd can be done as part of a related activity where contributors will receive a benefit from their participation. An example is the buyer/seller rating system on eBay. If a buyer in an eBay transaction rates the seller, there is greater likelihood that the seller will, in turn, rate the buyer who submitted the initial rating. This, in turn, can help both parties to establish a reputation for reliability that can enable them to participate more effectively in future transactions.

Some firms that elicit decisions or evaluations from the crowd, however, do this as a separate, stand-alone activity. Yelp, which publishes online rankings of restaurants, shops, and other locally based businesses, is one example. After more than a few dozen ratings have been submitted for any establishment, each individual contributor's ranking will do little, on its own, to change the overall ranking. This could reduce incentives to contribute—a phenomenon similar to the one identified by political scientists when they note that knowing in advance that many people are likely to cast ballots in an election can be a disincentive to vote (Downs 1957). One way Yelp encourages participation in the face of an individual's minuscule impact on overall ratings is by publishing the text of every review submitted by every user on its site, accompanied by each user's star rating, and with the user's name attached. Yelp also relies on other features that provide contributors with a sense of voice, such as allowing users to create home pages that feature a profile and all their reviews and by naming members who write many reviews to the site's "Elite Squad."

Collective Intelligence and Risk for Start-Ups

In view of the advantages that reliance on crowds can confer, one of the biggest risks for start-up ventures would be *not* to consider seriously the use of the crowd where possible. Reliance on the crowd is certainly not appropriate in all settings, but given the new possibilities opened up by web-enabled collective intelligence, entrepreneurs will at the very least want to think quite carefully about potential ways to incorporate the crowd in their new ventures.

At the same time, while the crowd may seem to offer significant benefits—including the prospect of tapping into a highly diverse pool of contributors at potentially low costs—reliance on the crowd also carries risks. One considerable risk is that developing a community to the point where it reaches critical mass so its talents can be tapped is a sizeable challenge, one that involves far more than simply building a website and expecting that people will find it and begin to congregate there. Developing the kind of community base needed for effective crowd-based creation or decision-making requires significant effort. Many attempts to create such communities never reach critical mass and instead founder. Any entrepreneur who seeks to leverage the talents of the crowd should recognize the magnitude of the community building challenge.

The work of developing and managing a community charged with doing work that represents an important part of a firm's value chain may not appear to be a stretch for entrepreneurs accustomed to juggling the demands of many stake-holders, including customers, partners, employees, and investors. But the skills required to manage an industrial supply chain or even a complex ecosystem of part-ners (Dhanaraj and Parkhe 2006) are still different from those required to manage a sizeable crowd of individual contributors. Community management on the web remains more art than science, though scholars have begun to mine a decade plus of history (Preece and Schneiderman 2009) and also apply principles from the social sciences (Kraut and Resnick in press) in developing toolkits that can be used by entrepreneurs.

The past few years have seen the growing maturation of collective intelligence-based platforms that client firms, including start-ups, can use to tap the talents of already established online communities. Examples include TopCoder and InnoCentive, for complex tasks like software development and scientific problem solving; Amazon's Mechanical Turk and CrowdFlower for simpler tasks; and a range of other platforms, including such firms as LiveOps, Elance, and oDesk, that operate somewhere in between. These platforms can provide start-ups access to crowd-based creation and decision-making at lower cost and less risk than if the new venture tried to build a community of its own from scratch. Platforms like TopCoder and Mechanical Turk could thus become an important part of the entrepreneur's toolbox in the future.

Another risk of crowd-enabled start-ups arises from network effects, the obser-vation that the value of a network grows as the square of the number of participants. In many domains, network effects dominate, and there is room for only a few—or even one—competitor. For example, Flickr has emerged as the dominant site for online photo collections. Its competitor, Picasa, remains a distant second, despite being acquired by, and receiving major support from, Google. Given this, in new domains, there may eventually be room for only a few or even one major player, which means there are sizeable risks associated with being an also-ran. These risks may not be so apparent when one looks out and sees the many prominent collective intelli-gence systems present on today's web. But there is a considerable amount of survivor bias in our perceptions of web-enabled collective intelligence systems. We tend to be aware of the efforts that were successful enough to establish a strong position and gain mindshare. We simply do not recognize the many efforts that did not become dominant and faltered along the way—they effectively remain invisible to us. For example, at the time of Wikipedia's launch in 2000, there were as many as a dozen other groups launching competing online encyclopedias. Within a few years, Wikipedia became the clear leader and has gone on since then to become dominant in its niche. The other efforts are forgotten, except by a handful of researchers.

There are also risks associated with reliance on specific CI genes. Some firms have experienced a backlash against their use of the Contest gene, based on the argument that contests require people to work on spec—shorthand widely used by workers in freelance professions for work done on a speculative basis—with no guarantee of payment. The backlash against some contest sites in graphic design became so great that a group of designers founded a site of their own, No!Spec, to get their story out on the web (No!Spec 2011). In relying on contests, firms must craft a value proposition that keeps individual participants from feeling they are being taken advantage of as a source of cheap labor or being exploited in other ways.

Systems that rely on the crowd to contribute decisions and evaluations, especially those based on location, have particular challenges of their own. By inviting people to contribute to a crowd-based assessment of the quality of establishments in a particular geographic region, perhaps a city or metro area, such systems are effectively asking contributors to develop a type of civic resource that will be available to people who live in the region as well as visitors. A resource of this kind is likely to be viewed by contributors as a type of public good. But an entrepreneur who creates a for-profit business involving crowd creation of this kind of public resource will still need to generate revenues, and the profit-making imperative of the firm may conflict with the contributors' sense that they are creating a community resource. In part out of recognition of this dynamic, Yelp did not include advertising initially. Some time after the site's launch, when it did introduce advertising, the management team experienced backlash from some of its contributors.

The Yelp example illustrates a more general risk for entrepreneurs using crowd-based models—getting the right combination of incentives can be challenging. In particular, including Money in systems that also rely on Glory and Love genes may not increase motivation, but rather, in a seeming paradox, decrease it. This is an example of what economists call the crowding-out problem, first identified when British blood banks added a paid donation option to what had previously been a wholly voluntary system—only to find that donations declined (Titmuss 1972). Experimental economists and neuroscientists are beginning to unravel the complex reasons behind this seemingly paradoxical result (Bowles (2008) provides a summary and Gneezy et al. (2010) describe an intriguing application). For now, entrepreneurs will want to tread carefully when designing systems that combine multiple Why genes.

Another challenge of crowd decision sites can arise from lack of control over the content. A group of hotel owners was recently considering a lawsuit against Trip-Advisor, a crowd-based hotel rating site, over negative reviews (Stellin 2010). Conflicts can also arise for companies that rely on crowd-based evaluations when contributors submit negative reviews of establishments that also buy advertising on the site (DeLorenzo 2010).

IMPACT OF COLLECTIVE INTELLIGENCE ON VENTURE CAPITAL FIRMS

Web-enabled collective intelligence could have an impact on venture capital firms by making it possible for the crowd to play a role in two of the key activities where venture capitalists currently assume responsibility:

- screening and selecting ideas for new ventures;
- financing new ventures.

Potential Impact of Collective Intelligence on Screening and Selecting Ideas for New Ventures

Two recent developments have begun to inject the crowd into the innovation process at large corporations. IBM's Innovation Jam is a structured annual process in which the company invites all of its key stakeholders to contribute ideas for new products or process improvements. IBM's Jams initially involved employees only, but they were subsequently expanded to include customers and suppliers. Ideas get proposed and then go through a multi-stage screening process. Proposals that make it through the process are funded, with the expectation that some of them will become new products to be offered to IBM's customers or process improvements to be implemented internally (Bjelland and Wood 2008).

The process of idea generation and screening embodied in IBM's Jams has been embedded in software applications like Spigit and Imaginatik. These applications, often called ideation tools, are frequently combined with consulting services and are typically deployed as part of focused or ongoing efforts to develop innovative ideas inside large firms. The combination of software tools and associated processes allows employees, and sometimes other corporate stakeholders, to propose ideas, develop them, and select the most promising ones to launch as new products or to implement internally (Townsend 2008).

These crowd-based approaches are eminently applicable to the venture capital process, and there is already at least one VC firm that has applied them. Spencer Trask has developed a web-based collective intelligence platform, VenCorps, and has recruited a web-based community that uses the platform to find and nurture new ventures. VenCorps relies on a community comprising entrepreneurs, scientists, investors, and government officials. An open variant of the platform has also been used to address social problems like traffic congestion. And the VenCorps technology served as the basis for the U.S. Department of Education's Open Innovation Initiative, which elicited new ideas for improving American schools, connected innovators who were working on complementary concepts, and funded the most promising teams (Wise 2009; Tapscott and Williams 2010).

The difference between the approach taken by VenCorps and that of the typical venture capital firm can be seen by mapping the genome of the two organizations. A VC firm raises money because investors—either institutions such as pension funds

		What	**Who**	**Why**	**How**
Typical venture capital firm	Decide	To invest in VC fund	Investors	Money	Hierarchy
	Create	Ideas for new start-ups	Crowd of entrepreneurs	Money	Collection
	Decide	Which start-ups to invest in	VCs	Money	Hierarchy

Figure 8.3. Genome Map for Typical Venture Capital Firm

and endowments or wealthy individuals—decide to place some portion of their portfolio with the firm. Entrepreneurs continually develop ideas for new start-ups, and the VC firm evaluates these ideas and decides to invest in a selected few. The key actors are the investors, the pool of entrepreneurs—which has the characteristics of a crowd, though it is not as large as the crowds that can be assembled on the Internet—and the venture capitalists. This genome can be expressed as in Figure 8.3.

In contrast with the more traditional model, VenCorps relies on the crowd not only to help enrich the ideas initially developed by entrepreneurs, it also uses the crowd to provide guidance about which are the most promising and deserve investment. Based on crowd input, VenCorps then makes the final investment decision itself. The VenCorps genome is given in Figure 8.4.

The potential of collective intelligence has also been recognized by others in the new venture sector. For example, the 2010 MIT Venture Capital Conference ended with a session using a tool called IdeaStorm, designed to harness the collective intelligence of attendees at the meeting (MIT Venture Capital Conference 2010). A related development is Springwise, a crowdsourced website that finds and posts promising new business ideas.

		What	**Who**	**Why**	**How**
VenCorps	Decide	To invest in VC fund	Institutional investors	Money	Hierarchy
	Create	Ideas for new start-ups	Crowd of entrepreneurs with online crowd	Money	Collection
	Decide	Which start-ups are promising	Crowd	Money	Averaging
	Decide	VenCorps	VenCorps	Money	Hierarchy

Figure 8.4. Genome Map for VenCorps

Potential Impact of Collective Intelligence in the Funding of New Ventures

A development that could have an even greater impact on venture capital firms is the emergence of crowdfunding, where both the selection and funding functions are externalized to crowds. Crowdfunding has already been used for social ends, through sites like Kiva, which combines the principles of microfinance and crowdfunding to link small business owners in developing countries with donors (Hartley 2010). As of early 2011, Kiva had channeled nearly $200 million to more than a half a million small business owners.

The success of Kiva has spurred the development of numerous platforms that allow donors to pool small amounts of funding for organizations that promote social causes and for arts projects. Some of these platforms are based on a charitable donation model, while others rely on debt financing or even providing equity to donors (Cahalane 2011). Kickstarter, one of the most prominent arts crowdfunding platforms, has funded more than 400 projects since its founding in 2009, with a dozen projects raising more than $50,000 and one raising nearly $1 million (Wortham 2009). An interesting feature of Kickstarter is that donors do not expect to get paid back or receive equity, though they do receive something tangible in return from the artists they fund—a CD, DVD, or print or an invitation to a concert, screening, or gallery opening.

The potential of crowdfunding has begun to be recognized by actors in the new venture sector. Friends and family and angel investors have long helped to fund new ventures before they were ready for venture capital investment. Crowdfunding takes this concept and combines it with the concept of web-enabled social networks. Social investors pursuing double bottom-line returns—profit plus social impact—have also frequently used direct public offerings (DPOs) to fund new ventures. DPOs also involve some of the same principles as crowdfunding, though they typically involve fewer investors who are less widely dispersed (Gore 2009).

Several venture capital firms based on the principles of crowdfunding have been formed. Grow VC was founded in early 2010, and it facilitated funding for approximately 20 start-ups in its first year. Grow VC has also launched Grow VC India, in collaboration with an Indian partner, Springboard Ventures (Chaudhary 2011). ProFounder, based in Silicon Valley, and StartNext, based in Germany, were launched

		What	**Who**	**Why**	**How**
VC firm based on crowd-funding	Create	Ideas for new start-ups	Crowd of entrepreneurs	Money	Collection
	Decide	Which start-ups to invest in	Crowd of investors	Money	Market

Figure 8.5. Genome Map for VC Firm Based on Crowdfunding

after Grow VC and employ a similar model. Some of the crowdfunding platforms that initially focused exclusively on social or arts-related activities are now also beginning to fund for-profit start-up ventures.

Venture capital firms based on crowdfunding are perhaps an even more radical departure from the typical venture capital model, since they rely on the crowd not only to evaluate the ventures, but also to provide investment funds. This reliance carries with it a set of legal questions, and in the United States, securities regulations make some aspects of crowdfunding challenging (Lawton and Marom 2010). This genomic map is shown in Figure 8.5.

The use of collective intelligence in the development and selection of ideas for new ventures and the rise of crowdfunding could both have major implications for venture capital firms. In each case, the crowd may increasingly come to assume a role that was formerly the province of venture capitalists. Some venture capital firms may adopt these practices, and new entrants, such as Grow VC, dedicated to crowd-based approaches, which currently hold a niche position, could emerge as viable competitors to mainstream venture capital.

IN CONCLUSION

Web-enabled collective intelligence has the potential to reshape innovation in the early twenty-first century as profoundly as the emergence of the new venture sector reshaped innovation in the latter half of the twentieth century. In the 1950s, when Fairchild Semiconductor was founded, start-up companies and their funders must have seemed exotic, even unserious, to observers who looked out at them from inside the corporate labs that still dominated innovation in the mid-twentieth-century economy. In the same way, early experiments with web-enabled collective intelligence may well appear exotic to observers who see them from inside the new venture sector that has come to dominate innovation in recent decades. But these experiments only scratch the surface of the potential that collective intelligence has to unleash new modes of innovation.

In the face of these developments, entrepreneurs will want to seek ways to take advantage of collective intelligence-based approaches for undertaking work formerly done by the employees of start-up companies. And venture capital firms will want to track the ongoing diffusion of collective intelligence-enabled innovation and seek ways to incorporate the crowd in the activities of their portfolio companies and to experiment with collective intelligence as a tool for running their own businesses.

ACKNOWLEDGMENTS

The original work on the Collective Intelligence Genome was undertaken in collaboration with Thomas W. Malone of MIT and Chrysanthos Dellarocas of Boston University, with financial support provided by BT plc. Richard Lai of the Wharton School and George Herman and Greg Little of MIT also contributed to that effort, and Michael Hopkins of *Sloan Management Review* provided valuable editorial input. Particular thanks go to David Bodde for encouragement and insightful guidance in the preparation of this chapter.

REFERENCES

Bartlett, Christopher A. and Ghoshal, Sumantra (1993) "Beyond the M-form: Toward a Managerial Theory of the Firm," *Strategic Management Journal*, 14 (S2): 23–46.

Benkler, Yochai (2006) *The Wealth of Networks: How Social Production Transforms Markets and Freedom*. New Haven and London: Yale University Press.

Bjelland, Osvald M. and Chapman Wood, Robert (2008) "An Inside View of IBM's 'Innovation Jam'," *Sloan Management Review*, 50 (1) (Fall): 32–40.

Boudreau, Kevin J. and Lakhani, Karim R. (2009) "How to Manage Outside Innovation," *Sloan Management Review*, 50 (4) (Summer): 69–76.

Bowles, Samuel (2008) "Policies Designed for Self-Interested Citizens May Undermine 'The Moral Sentiments': Evidence from Economic Experiments," *Science*, 320 (5883) (June 20): 1605–1609.

Brandenburger, Adam and Nalebuff, Barry (1998) *Co-opetition*. New York: Doubleday.

Cahalane, Claudia (2011) "Social Funding for Social Enterprises," *Guardian*, February 1. Available at: www.guardian.co.uk/social-enterprise-network/2011/feb/01/social-funding-supporting-projects.

Chaudhary, Deepti (2011) "Crowdfunding Yet To Start Up," wsj.com, March 16, Deals India. Available at: http://online.wsj.com/article/SB10001424052748704662604576201910 365336814.html.

Cook, Scott (2008) "The Contribution Revolution: Letting Volunteers Build Your Business," *Harvard Business Review*, 86 (10) (October): 60–69.

DeLorenzo, Ike (2010) "Everyone's a Critic; Yelp and other Online Sites and their Cadre of Amateurs have sent Nervous Ripples through the Restaurant World," *Boston Globe*, June 2.

Dhanaraj, Charles and Parkhe, Arvind (2006) "Orchestrating Innovation Networks," *Academy of Management Review*, 31 (3): 659–669.

Downs, Anthony (1957) "An Economic Theory of Political Action in a Democracy," *The Journal of Political Economy*, 65 (2) (April): 135–150.

Florida, Richard L. and Kenney, Martin (1988) "Venture Capital-financed Innovation and Technological Change in the USA," *Research Policy*, 17 (3) (June): 119–137.

Gneezy, Ayelet, Gneezy, Uri, Nelson, Leif D. and Brown, Amber (2010) "Shared Social Responsibility: A Field Experiment in Pay-What-You-Want Pricing and Charitable Giving," *Science*, 329 (5989) (July 16): 325–327.

Gompers, Paul and Lerner, Josh (2001) "The Venture Capital Revolution," *Journal of Economic Perspectives*, 15 (2) (April 1): 145–168.

Gore, Jason (2009) "Direct Public Offerings," *Green Ladder Funding*. Available at: www.greenladderfunding.com/over-500k-dpos.

Gulley, Ned (2004) "In Praise of Tweaking: A Wiki-like Programming Contest," *Interactions*, 11, (3) (May): 18–23.

Haines, Margaret (1989) "Brunelleschi and Bureaucracy: The Tradition of Public Patronage at the Florentine Cathedral," *I Tatti Studies: Essays in the Renaissance*, 3 (January 1): 89–125.

Hartley, Scott (2010) "Kiva.org: Crowd-Sourced Microfinance & Cooperation in Group Lending." Harvard Berkman Center working paper. Available at: http://dash.harvard.edu/handle/1/3757699.

Hounshell, David A. and Kenly Smith, John (1988) *Science and Corporate Strategy: Du Pont R&D, 1902–1980*. Cambridge: Cambridge University Press.

Howe, Jeff (2009) *Crowdsourcing: Why the Power of the Crowd is Driving the Future of Business*. New York: Crown.

Jana, Reena (2009) "Local Motors: A New Kind of Car Company," *BusinessWeek: Innovation*, November 3. Available at: www.businessweek.com/innovate/content/oct2009/id20091028_848755.htm.

Kraut, Robert and Resnick, Paul (Eds.) (In press) *Evidence-based Social Design: Mining the Social Sciences to Build Online Communities*. Cambridge, MA: MIT Press.

Lawton, Kevin and Marom, Dan (2010) *The Crowdfunding Revolution: Social Networking Meets Venture Financing*. Seattle: CreateSpace.

Malone, Thomas W. (1997) "Is 'Empowerment' Just a Fad? Control, Decision-making, and Information Technology," *Sloan Management Review*, 38 (2) (Winter): 23–35.

Malone, Thomas W. (2006) "What is Collective Intelligence and What Will We Do About It?" Edited transcript of remarks presented at the official launch of the MIT Center for Collective Intelligence, October 13, Cambridge, MA. Available at: http://cci.mit.edu/about/MaloneLaunchRemarks.html.

Malone, Thomas W., Laubacher, Robert and Dellarocas, Chrysanthos (2010) "The Collective Intelligence Genome," *Sloan Management Review*, 51 (3) (Spring): 21–31.

MIT Venture Capital Conference (2010) "We are Excited to Introduce the VC Conference's First Ideastorm." November 18. Available at: www.mitvcconference.com/ideastorm.htm.

No!Spec (2011) FAQ About Spec Work. Available at: www.no-spec.com/faq.

Powell, Walter W. (1990) "Neither Market nor Hierarchy: Network Forms of Organization," *Research in Organizational Behavior*, 12: 295–336.

Preece, Jennifer and Schneiderman, Ben (2009) "The Reader-to-Leader Framework: Motivating Technology-Mediated Social Participation," *AIS Transactions on Human–Computer Interaction*, 1 (1) (March): 13–32.

Quinn, James Brian (1999) "Strategic Outsourcing: Leveraging Knowledge Capabilities," *Sloan Management Review*, 40 (4) (Summer): 9–21.

Reich, Leonard S. (2002) *The Making of American Industrial Research: Science and Business at GE and Bell, 1876–1926*. Cambridge: Cambridge University Press.

Robb, John (2011) "The Open Source Venture Project (Picture This)," *Global Guerillas*, January 5. Available at: http://globalguerrillas.typepad.com/globalguerrillas/2011/01/the-open-source-venture-project-picture-this.html.

Simchi-Levi, David, Kaminsky, Philip and Simchi-Levi, Edith (2003) *Designing and Managing the Supply Chain: Concepts, Strategies, and Case Studies*. New York: McGraw Hill Professional.

Stellin, Susan (2010) "Unpacking Complaints," *New York Times*, October 26.

Surowiecki, James (2004) *The Wisdom of Crowds: Why the Many Are Smarter Than the Few and How Collective Wisdom Shapes Business, Economies, Societies and Nations*. New York: Doubleday.

Tapscott, Don and Williams, Anthony D. (2008) *Wikinomics: How Mass Collaboration Changes Everything*. New York: Penguin.

Tapscott, Don and Williams, Anthony D. (2010) *Macrowikinomics: Rebooting Business and the World*. New York: Penguin.

Titmuss, Richard Morris (1972) *The Gift Relationship; from Human Blood to Social Policy*. New York: Vintage Books.

Townsend, Chris (2008) *The Rise of Innovation Management Tools*. Forester Research Report, July 14.

Wise, Sean (2009) Crossing the Seed Capital Chasm through a Community Collaborative Online Information Network. Presented at the Collaborative Innovation Networks Conference, October 8, Savannah, Georgia. Available at: http://savannah09.coinsconference.org.

Wortham, Jenna (2009) "A Few Dollars at a Time, Patrons Support Artists on the Web," *New York Times*, August 25. Available at: www.nytimes.com/2009/08/25/technology/start-ups/25kick.html?_r=1&em.

X Prize Foundation (2011) Incentivized Competition Heritage. Available at: www.xprize.org/x-prizes/incentivized-competition-heritage.

Author Biographies

David L. Bodde

Dr. David Bodde is a Professor of Engineering at the International Center for Automotive Research, Clemson University. Dr. Bodde serves on the Board of Directors of several publicly traded companies and privately held ventures. His professional experience includes Vice President of the Midwest Research Institute, Assistant Director of the U.S. Congressional Budget Office, and Deputy Assistant Secretary in the Department of Energy. He recently chaired the Environmental Management Board, advising the Department of Energy on the cleanup of the U.S. nuclear weapons complex, and the Advisory Council of the Electric Power Research Institute (EPRI).

Dr. Bodde holds the Doctor of Business Administration, Harvard University (1976); Master of Science degrees in nuclear engineering (1972) and management (1973), both from the Massachusetts Institute of Technology (MIT); and a BS from the United States Military Academy (1965). He served in the U.S. Army in Vietnam.

Philip Bromiley

Philip Bromiley (PhD, Carnegie-Mellon University) is a Dean's Professor in Strategic Management at the Merage School of University of California, Irvine. Previously he held the Curtis L. Carlson Chair in Strategic Management and chaired the Department of Strategic Management & Organization at the University of Minnesota. He has published widely on organizational decision-making and strategic risk-taking. He currently serves on the boards of *Strategic Management Journal, Journal of Management Studies*, and *Journal of Strategy and Management*.

Previously, he served on the editorial boards of the *Academy of Management Journal, Organization Science, Strategic Organization*, and the *Journal of Management*, and as associate editor for *Management Science*. His current research examines strategic decision-making, the behavioral foundations of strategic management research, and corporate risk-taking. He has published over 60 journal articles and book chapters as well as two books. His most recent book, *Behavioral Foundations for Strategic Management*, argues for a behavioral basis for scholarly theory in strategic management.

James A. Euchner

Jim Euchner is a partner with Princeton Growth Partners, a consulting firm that helps clients accelerate growth through innovation. Jim is also a Visiting Scientist at the MIT Sloan School of Management, where he is studying varieties of open innovation. Prior to his current roles, Jim was Vice President of Growth Strategy and Innovation at Pitney Bowes, Inc., where he was responsible for corporate strategy, innovation and R&D. Earlier in his career, Jim was Vice President of Network Systems IT at Bell Atlantic (now Verizon).

Jim is a co-founder of the MIT Innovation Laboratory, a consortium of companies focused on nurturing innovation in organizations. He is currently Editor in Chief of *Research-Technology Management*, the journal of the Industrial Research Institute. He was previously a member of the Technical Advisory Council of the FCC and a member of the Technical Advisory Board for the Institute for Research on Learning. Jim received his Master's degree from Princeton University and his Bachelor's degree from Cornell University, both in mechanical and aerospace engineering. He also holds an MBA from Southern Methodist University.

William B. Gartner

William B. Gartner is the Arthur M. Spiro Professor of Entrepreneurial Leadership at Clemson University. He is the 2005 winner of the Swedish Entrepreneurship Foundation International Award for outstanding contributions to entrepreneurship and small business research. His scholarship focuses on new venture creation from many different perspectives, methods, and datasets.

His quantitative studies use the Panel Study of Entrepreneurial Dynamics (PSED): a longitudinal sample of nascent entrepreneurs in the process of starting businesses. His qualitative research uses narrative methods and ideas to explore the kinds of stories that entrepreneurs tell about their business development and the ways that stories are used to transform ideas into ongoing businesses. He is the Editor and Publisher of *ENTER (Entrepreneurial Narrative, Theory, Ethnomethodology and Reflexivity)*, a journal that devotes each issue to exploring a specific entrepreneurial narrative through a variety of perspectives.

Robert Laubacher

Robert Laubacher is Research Scientist and Associate Director at MIT's Center for Collective Intelligence. His work there examines how the Internet is enabling new forms of large-scale, globally distributed collaboration.

Mr. Laubacher has published in *Harvard Business Review, Sloan Management Review*, the *Financial Times*, and many academic venues. He co-edited *Inventing the Organizations of the 21st Century* (MIT Press, 2003), a volume based on a multi-year research project at the MIT Sloan School of Management.

During his time at MIT, Mr. Laubacher has worked as a consultant to global corporations, start-up firms, and the organization practice of McKinsey & Company. He also served as executive producer of two independent feature films, *American Wake* (2004) and *Home Before Dark* (1997), which won the grand jury prize at the

Hamptons International Film Festival, and was author of *Lens on the Bay State* (2006), a study of film production in Massachusetts.

Jianwen Liao

Dr. Jianwen (Jon) Liao is an Associate Professor of Strategy and Entrepreneurship in the Stuart School of Business at Illinois Institute of Technology and also an Adjunct Professor of Strategy and Innovation at Cheung Kong Graduate School of Business (CKGSB) in Beijing. His professional experience spans North America and Asia. Previously, he held academic appointments at DePaul University, Peking University, Hong Kong University of Science and Technology and China European International Business School (CEIBS).

Professor Liao has been working closely with the Panel Study of Entrepreneurial Dynamics (PSED)—the first large-scale, longitudinal research of nascent entrepreneurs and venture creation in the United States. He is the author of more than 30 scholarly articles published in journals including *Strategic Entrepreneurship Journal, Journal of Business Venturing, Entrepreneurship Theory and Practice, Journal of Small Business Management, Small Business Economics,* and *Journal of High Tech Management Research*. His research paper was featured in *The Small Business Economy: A Report to the President, 2007*. He has won several awards for his research and teaching, including the research grant award from the U.S. Small Business Administration (2007, 2008) and the Excellence in Teaching Award in 2009 at Stuart.

Rita Gunther McGrath

Rita Gunther McGrath, a Professor of Strategy at Columbia Business School, is one of the world's leading experts on innovation and growth. Her book, *Discovery Driven Growth*, was named one of *BusinessWeek*'s best design and innovation books of 2009. Her methodology for business planning (originally published in a best-selling *Harvard Business Review* article) was cited by Clayton Christensen as an antidote to "innovation killers." In 2009, she was inducted as a Fellow of the Strategic Management Society, an honor accorded to those who have had a significant impact on the field.

Rita joined the faculty of Columbia Business School in 1993. Prior to life in academia, she was an IT director, worked in the political arena and founded two startups. Her PhD is from the Wharton School, University of Pennsylvania. She teaches MBA and Executive MBA courses, and is the Faculty Director for the Columbia Executive Education program *Leading Strategic Growth and Change*. She is currently on the editorial boards of the *Strategic Management Journal* and *The Academy of Management Review*.

Jeffrey Pfeffer

Jeffrey Pfeffer (www.jeffreypfeffer.com) serves as the Thomas D. Dee II Professor of Organizational Behavior at the Stanford Graduate School of Business where he has taught since 1979. Pfeffer is the author or co-author of 13 books on topics including power in organizations, managing people, evidence-based management (www.evidence-basedmanagement.com), and *The Knowing-Doing Gap*. His most recent book, *Power: Why Some People Have It—and Others Don't*, was published in September, 2010. Author of more than 125 articles and book chapters, Pfeffer has won numerous awards for his scholarly research.

Pfeffer has taught seminars in 34 countries and has been a visiting professor at Harvard Business School, London Business School, Singapore Management University, and IESE in Barcelona. Prior to joining Stanford, he was on the faculty at the business schools at the University of California, Berkeley, and the University of Illinois. Pfeffer has served on the board of directors of several human capital software companies as well as other public and non-profit boards.

Devaki Rau

Devaki Rau is an Associate Professor at the Department of Management at Northern Illinois University. She obtained her PhD in management from the University of Minnesota. Her research focuses on decision-making, top management teams, and the recognition and utilization of expertise in teams and individuals. Dr. Rau has published her research in journals such as the *Journal of Applied Psychology*, *Journal of Management*, and *Small Group Research*. She worked as a business development executive in CMC Ltd., a software development and maintenance firm in Bangalore, India, prior to obtaining her PhD.

Caron H. St. John

Dr. Caron H. St. John is Dean of the College of Business Administration at the University of Alabama, Huntsville. Previously, she was the Associate Dean of Graduate Programs, Research and Outreach in the College of Business & Behavioral Science at Clemson University, with responsibility for MBA programs, Executive Education programs, the Spiro Institute for Entrepreneurial Leadership, and the Small Business Development Center.

Dr. St. John has served as the PI or Co-PI on grants from the National Science Foundation and U.S. Department of Commerce totaling over $1.5 million and has published research in leading management journals including the *Academy of Management Review*, *Strategic Management Journal*, *Journal of Operations Management*, *Organization Research Methods*, *Computers and Operations Research*, and *Production and Operations Management*. She received her undergraduate degree in chemistry from Georgia Institute of Technology and a MBA and PhD in business administration from Georgia State University. Before pursuing an academic career, she was involved in new product and new business development with Celanese Corporation in Charlotte, NC.

John T. Wilbanks

John Wilbanks works on open content, open data, and open innovation systems in the life sciences and sustainability. He has worked at Creative Commons, the Berkman Center for Internet & Society at Harvard University, MIT's Computer Science and

Artificial Intelligence Laboratory, the World Wide Web Consortium, and the U.S. House of Representatives. He started a bioinformatics company called Incellico, which is now part of Selventa. John sits on the Board of Directors for Sage Bionetworks, AcaWiki, and 1DegreeBio, as well as the Advisory Board for Boundless Learning, and serves as a mentor at RockHealth. He is a member of the Global Agenda Council on sustainable consumption for the World Economic Forum among other industry and national research boards. He studied philosophy and French at Tulane University and modern letters at the Sorbonne.

Index